Priase for "Who Said Jews Aren't Funny?"

VERY FUNNY!

"You're **Gonna** Laugh"

WHO SAID JEWS AREN'T FUNNY?

Over 330 of the Funniest Jewish Jokes Ever

A Compilation by Sandy Rozelman

Second Edition

I received this book as a gift. I just started reading it. I didn't expect it to be as funny as it is. I've done some stand-up comedy and know a lot of jokes, but there are many in this book that I have never heard before. It's a VERY good compilation of Jewish jokes. In fact, many can be read as if they are from any religious background, but most are strictly Jewish. I found myself telling the jokes to friends and then telling them about the book, so I decided I should write this review and let everyone know that this is a very funny book. I open it up everyday now and read a few jokes to get a good laugh. What will I do when I'm finished? I guess I'll have to get another one of Sandy's other funny books. Great job Sandy. Thank you, for all of the laughs that I've had and will have from your book!

I highly recommend this book to everyone that enjoys a good joke. As Sandy says on the cover… "You will laugh."

I give this book a very solid 5 out of 5 STARS!

—Talbot Perry Simons, CEO
American Patriot Pictures, LLC
Guinness World Records® most awarded filmmaker in the world for the movie *Still the Drums*

Politics
IS A
Joke

Skipp,
Enjoy some humor
during this crazy
election year!
Gundy Rozek

You're Gonna Laugh

Politics

Is A

Joke

Sandy Rozelman

TATE PUBLISHING
AND ENTERPRISES, LLC

Published by Tate Publishing & Enterprises, LLC
127 E. Trade Center Terrace | Mustang, Oklahoma 73064 USA
1.888.361.9473 | www.tatepublishing.com

Tate Publishing is committed to excellence in the publishing industry. The company reflects the philosophy established by the founders, based on Psalm 68:11,
"The Lord gave the word and great was the company of those who published it."

Book design copyright © 2013 by Tate Publishing, LLC. All rights reserved.
Cover design by Rtor Maghuyop
Interior design by Ronnel Luspoc

Published in the United States of America

ISBN: 978-1-62295-065-2
1. Humor / General
2. Humor / Topic / Political
12.11.26

Table of Contents

Acknowledgments

Many thanks to all of my e-mail buddies for sending me all the jokes. Keep them coming!

This is for all of you serious people who don't see anything funny about politics. I'm here to prove you wrong and to make you laugh.

A special thank you to my husband, Joe, for all his love, support and encouragement to get this done.

Introduction

Politics is a Joke covers the Bush, Clinton, Bush, and Obama era with a few others thrown in for good measure and, of course, a laugh.

As with my first two books, *'You're Gonna Laugh'* and *'Who Said Jews Aren't Funny?'*, all of the jokes in this book were e-mailed to me over the last fifteen years. I saved them all until this year, when, because it was an election year, I wanted to share the fun with everyone.

Humor is making fun of the truth and the truth isn't always pretty, but it's almost always funny.

—An original quote by Sandy Rozelman

The Laugh Heard Around the World

The Pentagon announced today the formation of a new 500-man elite fighting unit called the United States Redneck Special Forces (USRSF).

These West Virginia boys will be dropped off into Iraq and have been given only the following facts about terrorists:

1. The season opened today.

2. There is no limit.

3. They taste just like chicken.

4. They don't like beer, pickups, country music, or Jesus.

5. They are directly responsible for the death of Dale Earnhardt.

The Pentagon expects the problem in Iraq to be over by Friday.

———★———

Two opposing politicians were sharing a rare moment together. The Liberal politician said, "I never pass up a chance to promote the party. For example, whenever I take a cab, I give the driver a sizable tip and say, 'Vote Liberal.'"

His opponent said, "I have a better scheme, and it doesn't cost me a nickel. I don't give any tip at all. And when I leave, I also say, 'Vote Liberal.'"

———★———

Illegal aliens have always been a problem in the United States. Ask any Indian.

———★———

A plane is about to crash. There are five passengers on board, but there are only four parachutes.

The first passenger says, "I am Lebron James, the best basketball player in the world. The sports world needs me, and I cannot die on my fans." He grabs the first parachute and jumps out of the plane.

The second passenger, Hillary Clinton says, "I am the wife of the former president of the United States. I am the senator of New York, and I have a good chance of being president of the United States in the future." She grabs a parachute and jumps off the plane.

The third passenger, George W. Bush, says, "I am the president of the United States of America. I have huge responsibilities in the world. Besides, I am the smartest president in the history of my country and can't shun the responsibility to my people by dying."

The fourth passenger, the Pope, says to the fifth passenger, a young schoolboy, "I am old. I have lived my life as a good person as a priest should and so I shall leave the last parachute to you. You have the rest of your life ahead of you."

To this the little boy says, "Don't fret, old man. There is a parachute for each of us! The smartest president in America just grabbed my backpack."

———★———

A lot of folks can't understand how we came to have an oil shortage here in our country.

Well, there's a very simple answer.

Nobody bothered to check the oil.

We just didn't know we were getting low.

The reason for that is purely geographical.

Our *oil* is located in Alaska, California, Coastal Florida, Coastal Louisiana, Kansas, Oklahoma, Pennsylvania, and Texas.

Our *dipsticks* are located in Washington, DC.

———★———

Albert Einstein, Pablo Picasso, and George W. Bush have all died. Due to a glitch in the mundane/celestial time-space continuum, all three arrive at the pearly gates more or less simultaneously, even though their deaths have taken place decades apart. The first to present himself to Saint Peter is Einstein. At the pearly gates, Saint Peter tells him, "You look like Einstein, but you have no idea the lengths that some people will go to, to sneak into heaven. Can you prove who you really are?"

Einstein ponders for a second and asks for a blackboard and some chalk. He proceeds to describe with arcane mathematics and symbols his theory of relativity.

Saint Peter is impressed and says, "Welcome to heaven!"

Picasso is next to arrive, and once again Saint Peter asks for credentials. Picasso picks up the chalk and sketches a truly stunning mural. Saint Peter says, "Surely you are the great artist you claim to be. Come on in!"

Saint Peter looks up and sees George W. Bush and says, "Einstein and Picasso both managed to prove their identity. How can you prove yours?"

George W. looks bewildered and says, "Who are Einstein and Picasso?"

"Come on in, George."

———★———

I don't approve of political jokes. I've seen too many of them get elected.

———★———

And can our politicians be devoted? We can only hope!

———★———

Politics is supposed to be the second oldest profession. I have come to realize that it bears a very close resemblance to the first.

If a lawyer and an IRS agent were both drowning, and you could only save one of them, would you go to lunch or read the newspaper?

———★———

The post office just recalled their newest stamps. They had pictures of IRS agents on them, and people couldn't figure out which side to spit on.

———★———

One girl to another: "What I'm looking for is a man who will treat me as if I was a voter and he was a candidate."

———★———

President Bush was invited to address a major gathering of the American Indian Nation last weekend in Arizona. He spoke for almost an hour on his future plans for increasing every Native American's present standard of living. He referred to his career as governor of Texas, how he had signed 1,237 times—for every Indian issue that came to his desk for approval. Although the president was vague on the details of his plan, he seemed most enthusiastic about his future ideas for helping his "red brothers."

At the conclusion of his speech, the tribes presented the president with a plaque inscribed with his new Indian name—Walking Eagle. The proud president then departed in his motorcade, waving to the crowds.

A news reporter later inquired to the group of chiefs of how they came to select the new name given to the president. They explained that Walking Eagle is the name given to a bird so full of crap it can no longer fly.

—★—

The reason congressmen try so hard to get re-elected is that they would hate to have to make a living under the laws they've passed.

—★—

Iraqi Humor

Q: What is the Iraqi air force motto?
A: I came, I saw, Iran.

Q: Have you heard about the new Iraqi Air Force exercise program?
A: Each morning you raise your hands above your head and leave them there.

Q: What's the five-day forecast for Baghdad?
A: Two days.

Q: What do Miss Muffet and Saddam Hussein have in common?
A: They both have Kurds in their way.

Q: What is the best Iraqi job?
A: Foreign ambassador.

Q: Did you hear that it is twice as easy to train Iraqi fighter pilots?

A: You only have to teach them to take off.

Q: How do you play Iraqi bingo?
A: A-6...B-52...F-16...B-52

Q: What is Iraq's national bird?
A: Duck.

Q: What do Saddam Hussein and General Custer have in common?
A: They both want to know where the hell those Tomahawks are coming from!

Q: Why does the Iraqi navy have glass bottom boats?
A: So they can see their air force.

———★———

IRS Humor

Sometimes all we can do is laugh when we think about the antics of the IRS. Here are a few jokes that levy a tax of great humor at the expense of IRS agents!

Q: What do you call twenty-five IRS agents buried up to their chins in cement?
A: Not enough cement.

Q: What do you call twenty-five skydiving IRS agents?
A: Skeet.

Q: What do you throw to a drowning IRS agent?
A: His co-workers.

Q: What's brown and looks really good on an I.R.S. agent?
A: A Doberman.

Q: What's the difference between an IRS agent and a mosquito?
A: One is a bloodsucking parasite; the other is an insect.

——★——

Bill and Hillary were going down a back road and stopped at a gas station. As the worker was filling up their car, he said to Hillary, "I went to high school with you."

She recognized him and agreed with him. Later as they were driving down the road Bill said, "If you had married him you wouldn't be married to the president."

Hillary said, "Oh, yes I would! He would be president."

——★——

Hillary Clinton died and, Lord knows why, went to heaven. St. Peter approached her and says, "Hillary, I know you're 'somebody' down on Earth, but up here, you're just another person. And I'm swamped right now, so have a seat and I'll get back with you as soon as I can."

So Hillary sits down and begins looking at her surroundings. She notices a huge wall that extends as far as the eye can see. And on that wall there are millions and millions of clocks. She can't help notice that on occasion some of the clocks jump ahead fifteen minutes.

When St. Peter returns she asks, "What's with the clocks?"

St. Peter replies, "There is a clock on the wall for every married man on Earth."

Hillary asks, "Well, what does it mean when the clock jumps ahead fifteen minutes?"

St. Peter replies, "That means that the man that belongs to that clock has just committed adultery."

Hillary asks, "Well, is my husband's clock on the wall?"

St. Peter replies, "Of course not. God has it in his office and is using it for an electric fan."

———★———

A shipwrecked mariner had spent several years on a deserted island when one day he was thrilled to see a ship offshore and a smaller vessel pulling out toward him.

When the boat grounded on the beach, the officer in charge handed the marooned sailor a bundle of newspapers and told him, "With the captain's compliments. He said to read through these and let us know if you still want to be rescued."

Democracy means that anyone can grow up to be president and anyone who doesn't grow up can be vice president.

———★———

An Indian walks into a cafe with a shotgun in one hand pulling a male buffalo with the other. He says to the waiter:

"Want coffee."

The waiter says, "Sure, Chief. Coming right up." He gets the Indian a tall mug of coffee. The Indian drinks the coffee down in one gulp, turns and blasts the buffalo with the shotgun, causing parts of the animal to splatter everywhere and then just walks out. The next morning the Indian returns. He has his shotgun in one hand, pulling another male buffalo with the other. He walks up to the counter and says to the waiter: "Want coffee."

The waiter says "Whoa, Tonto! We're still cleaning up your mess from yesterday. What was all that about, anyway?"

The Indian smiles and proudly says: "Training for position in United States Congress: Come in, drink coffee, shoot the bull, leave mess for others to clean up, disappear for rest of day."

———★———

Why does a slight tax increase cost you 200 dollars and a substantial tax cut save you thirty cents?

George W. Bush, in an airport lobby, noticed a man in a long, flowing, white robe with a long, flowing, white beard and flowing white hair. The man had a staff in one hand and some stone tablets under the other arm.

George W. approached the man and inquired, "Aren't you Moses?" The man ignored George W. and stared at the ceiling. George W. positioned himself more directly in the man's view and asked again, "Aren't you Moses?"

The man continued to peruse the ceiling. George W. tugged at the man's sleeve and asked once again, "Aren't you Moses?" The man finally responded in an irritated voice, "Yes, I am."

George W. asked him why he was so unfriendly, and Moses replied, "The last time I spoke to a Bush I had to spend forty years in the desert."

———★———

Two men were stopped by a TV newswoman doing street interviews about the upcoming presidential election.

"I'm not voting for any of the candidates," the first man said. "I don't know any of them."

"I feel the same way," the second man said. "Only I know them all."

———★———

George W. Bush was asked by a reporter what he thought of *Roe vs. Wade*. He said, "I don't care what method the people use to get out of New Orleans."

George W. Bush was very depressed that people were saying he is stupid. So he calls his good friend Queen Elizabeth, who says, "Now, George, what you need to do is to surround yourself with smart people. Let me show you." She calls Tony Blair in and asks, "Tony, your parents had a baby. It isn't your sister and it isn't your brother. Who is it?"

Tony Blair replies, "It's me!"

So G.W. calls Dick Cheney and says, "Dick, your parents had a baby. It isn't your sister and it isn't your brother. Who is it?"

And Cheney says, "Wow, that's a tough one. Let me get back to you."

So Cheney calls Colin Powell and says, "Colin, your parents had a baby. It isn't your sister and it isn't your brother. Who is it?"

And Colin Powell says, "It's me!"

So Cheney calls Bush and says, "It's Colin Powell."

And Bush says, "No, you idiot! It's Tony Blair!"

——★——

George W. Bush was asked if he knew what *Roe vs. Wade* was about, and he answered that he thought it was the decision George Washington had to make when he decided to cross the Delaware.

——★——

When President George W. Bush was asked "Why are you so sure that Iraq has weapons of mass destruction?" he answered, "Easy, we kept the receipts."

Bush and Cheney are having lunch at a diner near the White House. Cheney orders the "Heart-Healthy" salad.

Bush leans over to the waitress and says, "Honey, could I have a quickie?"

She's horrified! She says, "Mr. President, I thought your administration would bring a new era of moral rectitude to the White House. Now I see I was wrong, and I'm sorry I voted for you." And she marches off.

Cheney leans over and says, "George, I think it's pronounced 'quiche'."

—★—

A tragic fire on Tuesday night destroyed the personal library of President George W. Bush. Both of his books have been lost. A presidential spokesman said that the president was devastated, as he had not finished coloring the second one.

—★—

The latest telephone poll taken by the Florida governor's office asked whether people who live in Florida think illegal immigration is a serious problem:

Twenty-nine percent of respondents answered: "Yes, it is a serious problem."

Seventy-one percent of respondents answered: "No, es una problema seriosa."

Everyone concentrates on the problems we're having in this country lately: illegal immigration, hurricane recovery, wild animals attacking humans in Florida. Here is a solution to all the problems. The result is a win-win-win situation:

Dig a moat the length of the Mexican border.

Use the dirt to raise the levies in New Orleans.

Put the Florida alligators in the moat.

———★———

The eight Saddam body doubles are gathered in one of the bunkers in downtown Baghdad. Tariq Aziz, the deputy prime minister, comes in and says, "I have some good news and some bad news."

They ask for the good news first.

Aziz says, "The good news is that Saddam is still alive, so you all still have jobs."

"And the bad news?" they ask.

Aziz replies, "He's lost an arm."

———★———

Forty-three percent of all Americans polled said that immigration is a serious problem. The other 57 percent said, "No hablo ingles."

———★———

President George W. Bush is visiting an elementary school class. They are in the middle of a discussion related to words and their meanings. The teacher asks the President if he would like to lead the class in the discussion of the word *tragedy*. So the illustrious leader asks the class for an example of a tragedy.

One little boy stands up and offers, "If my best friend, who lives next door, is playing in the street and a car comes along and runs him over, that would be a tragedy."

"No," says Bush, "that would be an accident."

A little girl raises her hand: "If a school bus carrying fifty children drove off a cliff, killing everyone involved, that would be a tragedy."

"I'm afraid not," explains Mr. President. "That's what we would call a great loss."

The room goes silent. No other children volunteer. President Bush searches the room. "Isn't there someone here who can give me an example of a tragedy?"

Finally, way in the back of the room, a small boy raises his hand. In a quiet voice he says, "If Air Force One, carrying Mr. Bush, was struck by a missile and blown up to smithereens, by a terrorist like Osama bin Laden; that would be a tragedy."

"Fantastic," exclaims Bush, "that's right. And can you tell me why that would be a tragedy?"

"Well," says the boy, "because it wouldn't be an accident, and it certainly wouldn't be a great loss."

——★——

Seen on an infant's shirt: "Already smarter than Bush."

What is the difference between Clinton and the Titanic?
More women went down on Clinton.

—★—

When Ariel Sharon came to Washington last year for meetings with George W. and for a state dinner, Laura Bush decided to bring in a special kosher chef and offer a truly Jewish meal. At the dinner that night, the first course served is matzo ball soup. George W. looks at this, and after learning what it is called he tells an aide that he can't eat such a gross and strange-looking brew. The aide says that Mr. Sharon will be insulted if he doesn't at least taste it.

Not wanting to cause any trouble (after all, he ate sheep's eye in honor of Arab guests), George W. gingerly lowers his spoon into the bowl and retrieves a piece of matzo ball and some broth; he hesitates, then swallows. A big grin appears on his face. He finds that he really likes it, so he digs right in and finishes the whole bowl.

"That was delicious," Bush says to Sharon. "Do you Jews eat any other part of the matzo, or just the balls?"

—★—

Bumper Stickers We'd Like To See

We've all seen interesting bumper stickers plastered on the backs of cars. People are no longer content to express themselves through the make, model, and color of theirs cars; they have to have stickers! In bright colors! That let the whole world know what they're thinking! Here are a few stickers that might make you crack a smile on the way to work.

- 1/20/09: End of an Error

- That's okay, I Wasn't Using My Civil Liberties Anyway

- Let's Fix Democracy in This Country First

- If You Want a Nation Ruled By Religion, Move to Iran

- Bush. Like a Rock. Only Dumber.

- You Can't Be Pro-War And Pro-Life At The Same Time

- If You Can Read This, You're Not Our President

- Of Course It Hurts: You're Getting Screwed by an Elephant

- Hey, Bush Supporters: Embarrassed Yet?

- George Bush: Creating the Terrorists Our Kids Will Have to Fight

- Impeachment: It's Not Just for Blow jobs Anymore

- America: One Nation, Under Surveillance

- They Call Him "W" So He Can Spell It

- Which God Do You Kill For?

- Jail to the Chief

- No, Seriously, Why Did We Invade??

- Bush: God's Way of Proving Intelligent Design is Full Of Crap

- Bad president! No Banana.

- We Need a President Who's Fluent In At Least One Language

- We're Making Enemies Faster Than We Can Kill Them

- Rich Man's War, Poor Man's Blood

- Is It Vietnam Yet?

- Bush Doesn't Care About White People, Either

- Where Are We Going? And Why Are We In This Hand Basket?

- You Elected Him. You Deserve Him.

- When Bush Took Office, Gas Was $1.46

———★———

How come we choose from just two people for president and fifty for Miss America?

Hillary is changing the name of her book to: *It Takes a Village to Satisfy My Husband.*

———★———

What is one billion?

According to a recent government publication…A billion seconds ago Harry Truman was president. A billion minutes ago was just after the time of Christ. A billion hours ago man had not yet walked on Earth. A billion dollars ago was late yesterday at the U.S. Treasury.

———★———

A little girl asked her father, "Daddy? Do all fairytales begin with 'Once Upon A Time'?"

He replied, "No, there is a whole series of fairytales that begin with 'If elected I promise'."

———★———

Little David comes home from first grade and tells his father that they learned about the history of Valentine's Day. "Since Valentine's Day is for a Christian saint and we're Jewish, will God get mad at me for giving someone a valentine?"

"No, I don't think God would get mad," answered his father. "Who do you want to give a valentine to?"

"Osama Bin Laden."

"Why Osama Bin Laden?" his father asks in shock.

"Well, I thought that if a little American Jewish boy could have enough love to give Osama a valentine, he might start to think that maybe we're not all that bad and maybe start loving people a little bit. And if other kids saw what I did and sent valentines to Osama, he'd love everyone a lot. And then he'd start going all over the place to tell everyone how much he loved them and how he didn't hate anyone anymore."

His father's heart swells, and he looks at his son with newfound pride. "David, that's the most wonderful thing I've ever heard."

"I know," David says. "And once that gets him out in the open, the Marines could blow the crap out of him."

———★———

The Saudi Ambassador to the U.N. has just finished giving a speech and walks out into the lobby where he meets his American counterpart. They shake hands and as they walk the Saudi ambassador says, "You know, I have just one question about what I have seen in America."

The American says, "Well, Your Excellency, anything I can do to help you I will do."

The Saudi ambassador whispers, "My son watches this show *Star Trek* and in it there are Russians and blacks and Asians, but never any Arabs. He is very upset. He doesn't understand why there are never any Arabs in *Star Trek*."

The American laughs and leans over. "That's because it takes place in the future."

A young man married a beautiful woman who had previously divorced ten husbands. On their wedding night, she told her new husband, "Please be gentle. I'm still a virgin."

"What?" said the puzzled groom. "How can that be if you've been married ten times?"

"Well, husband number one was a sales representative. He kept telling me how great it was going to be."

"Husband number two was in software services. He was never really sure how it was supposed to function, but he said he'd look into it and get back to me."

"Husband number three was from field services. He said everything checked out diagnostically, but he just couldn't get the system up."

"Husband number four was in telemarketing. Even though he knew he had the order, he didn't know when he would be able to deliver."

"Husband number five was an engineer. He understood the basic process but wanted three years to research, implement, and design a new state-of-the-art method."

"Husband number six was from administration. He thought he knew how, but he wasn't sure whether it was his job or not."

"Husband number seven was in marketing. Although he had a product, he was never sure how to position it."

"Husband number eight was a psychiatrist. All he ever did was talk about it."

"Husband number nine was a gynecologist. All he did was look."

"Husband number ten was a stamp collector. All he ever did was...God, I miss him! But now that I've married you, I'm so excited!"

"Wonderful," said the husband, "but, why?"

"You're with the government...this time I know I'm gonna get screwed."

—★—

Headlines from the year 2029!

Who knows what the future holds? There are plenty of people who are confident they can predict what's around the corner. Here are some thoughts on what the newspapers of the future might be declaring:

- Ozone created by electric cars now killing millions in the seventh largest country in the world, Mexifornia, formerly known as California.

- White minorities still trying to have English recognized as Mexifornia's third language.

- Baby conceived naturally—scientists stumped.

- Couple petitions court to reinstate heterosexual marriage.

- Iran still closed off; physicists estimate it will take at least ten more years before radioactivity decreases to safe levels.

- France pleads for global help after being taken over by Jamaica.

- Castro finally dies at age 112; Cuban cigars can now be imported legally, but President Chelsea Clinton has banned all smoking.

- George Z. Bush says he will run for president in 2036.

- Average weight of Americans drops to 250 pounds.

- Postal Service raises price of first class stamp to $17.89 and reduces mail delivery to Wednesdays only.

- Eighty-five-year, $75.8 billion study: diet and exercise is the key to weight loss.

- Japanese scientists have created a camera with such a fast shutter speed, they now can photograph a woman with her mouth shut.

- Massachusetts executes last remaining conservative.

- Supreme Court rules punishment of criminals violates their civil rights.

- Average height of NBA players now nine feet, seven inches.

- IRS sets lowest tax rate at 75 percent!

- Florida voters still having trouble with voting machines.

Section 2

A shepherd was tending his flock in a remote pasture when suddenly a brand-new Jeep Cherokee appeared out of a dust cloud, advanced toward him and stopped. The driver, a twenty-four-year-old young man wearing an Armani suit, Gucci shoes, Ray Ban sunglasses, and a YSL tie, leaned out of the window and asked our shepherd, "If I can tell you exactly how many sheep you have in your flock, will you give me one?"

The shepherd looked at the young guy, then at his peacefully grazing flock, and calmly answered, "Sure."

The young man parked his car, whipped out his notebook computer, connected it to a cell phone, surfed to a NASA page on the Internet where he called up a GPS satellite navigation system, scanned the area, then opened up a database and some Excel spreadsheets with complex formulas. He finally printed out a 150-page report on his high-tech miniaturized printer, turned around to our shepherd and said, "You have here exactly 1,586 sheep!"

"Amazing! That's correct! Like I agreed, you can take one of my sheep," said the shepherd.

The shepherd watched the man make a selection and bundle it into his Cherokee. When he was finished the sheepherder said, "If I can tell you exactly what your political persuasion is, where you're from and whom you work for, will you give me my sheep back?"

"Okay, why not," answered the young man.

"You're a Democrat from Palm Beach, and you're working for Jesse Jackson," said the shepherd.

"Wow! That's correct," said the young man. "How did you ever guess that?" "Easy," answered the shepherd, "nobody called you, but you showed up here anyway. You want to be paid for providing a solution to a question I already knew the answer to. And, you don't know squat about what you're doing because you just took my dog."

———★———

A little boy who wanted $100 very badly prayed and prayed for two weeks, but nothing happened. Then he decided to write a letter to God requesting the $100. When the postal authorities received the letter to "God, USA," they decided to send it to President Bush.

The president was so impressed, touched, and amused that he asked his secretary to send the little boy a five-dollar bill. He thought this would appear to be a lot of money to a little boy.

The little boy was delighted with the five dollars and immediately sat down to write a thank you note to God.

"Dear, God, thank you for sending me the money. However, I noticed that for some reason you had to send it through Washington, D.C., and as usual, they deducted ninety-five dollars!"

———★———

A priest walked into a barbershop in Washington, D.C. After he got his haircut he asked how much it would be. The barber said, "No charge. I consider it a service to the Lord."

The next morning the barber came to work and there were twelve prayer books and a thank you note from the priest in the front door.

Later that day a police officer came in and got his haircut. When he asked how much he owed, the barber said, "No charge. I consider it a service to the community."

The next morning he came to work, and there were a dozen donuts and a thank you note from the police officer.

Then a senator came in and got a haircut. When he was done he asked how much it was. The barber said, "No charge. I consider it a service to the country."

The next morning when the barber got to work there were twelve senators waiting at the door.

———★———

A little boy asks his dad, "Daddy, what is politics?"

His dad says, "Well, son, let me try to explain it this way: I'm the breadwinner of the family, so let's call me Capitalism. Your mom, she's the administrator of the money, so we'll call her the Government. We're here to take care of your needs, so we'll call you People. The Nanny, we'll consider her the Working Class. Your baby brother, we'll call him the Future. Now think about that and see if that makes sense."

So the little boy goes off to bed thinking about what his dad had said. Later that night he hears his baby brother crying so he gets up to check on him. He finds that the baby has severely pooped in his diaper. So the little boy goes to his parents' room and finds his mother sound asleep. Not wanting to wake her, he goes to the Nanny's room. Finding the door locked, he peeks in the keyhole and sees his father getting it on with her. He gives up and goes back to bed.

The next morning the little boy says to his father, "Dad, I think I understand the concept of politics now."

"Excellent, my boy, what have you learned?"

"Well, while Capitalism is screwing the Working Class, the Government is asleep, the People are being ignored and the Future is in deep s—t."

———★———

Politicians and diapers have one thing in common. They should both be changed regularly and for the same reason.

———★———

Two Iraqi spies met in a busy restaurant after they had successfully slipped into the United States.

The first spy starts speaking in Arabic.

The second spy hushes him quickly and whispers: "Don't blow our cover. You're in America now. Speak Spanish!"

———★———

George Bush was out jogging one morning when he tripped, fell over the bridge railing, and landed in the creek below. Before the Secret Service guys could get to him, three kids, who were fishing, pulled him out of the water. He was so grateful he offered the kids whatever they wanted.

The first kid said, "I sure would like to go to Disneyland." George said, "I'll take you there on Air Force One."

The second kid said, "I really need a new pair of Nike Air Jordan's."

George said, "I'll get them for you and even have Michael sign them!"

The third kid said, "I want a motorized wheelchair with a built-in TV and stereo headset!"

George Bush is a little perplexed by this and says, "But you don't look like you are injured."

The kid says, "I will be after my dad finds out I saved your ass from drowning!"

———★———

A state government employee sits in his office and out of boredom, decides to see what's in his old filing cabinet. He pokes through the contents and comes across an old brass lamp.

"This will look great on my mantelpiece," he decides and takes it home with him. While polishing the lamp, a genie appears and grants him three wishes.

"I wish for an ice cold beer right now!"

Poof! He gets his beer and drinks it. Now that he can think more clearly, he states his second wish.

"I wish to be on an island where beautiful nymphomaniacs reside."

Poof! Suddenly he is on an island with gorgeous women eyeing him lustfully. He tells the genie his third and last wish:

"I wish I'd never have to work again."Poof! He's back in his government office."

———★———

State Mottos

Every state has something to brag about, whether it's their weather, their exports, their economy, or their friendliness. Here's a humorous look at what the true motto of each state should be:

Alabama: Hell Yes, We Have Electricity
Alaska: 11,623 Eskimos Can't Be Wrong!
Arizona: But It's A Dry Heat
Arkansas: Literacy Ain't Everything
California: By Thirty, Our Women Have More Plastic Than Your Honda
Colorado: If You Don't Ski, Don't Bother
Connecticut: Like Massachusetts, Only The Kennedy's Don't Own It—Yet
Delaware: We Really Do Like The Chemicals In Our Water
Florida: Ask Us About Our Grandkids
Georgia: We Put The "Fun" In Fundamentalist Extremism
Hawaii: Haka Tiki Mou Sha'ami Leeki Toru (Death To Mainland Scum, But Leave Your Money)

Idaho: More Than Just Potatoes...Well Okay, We're Not, But The Potatoes Sure Are Real Good

Illinois: Please Don't Pronounce the "S"

Indiana: Two Billion Years Tidal Wave Free

Iowa: We Do Amazing Things With Corn

Kansas: First of The Rectangle States

Kentucky: Five Million People; Fifteen Last Names

Louisiana: We're Not All Drunk Cajun Wackos, But That's Our Tourism Campaign

Maine: We're Really Cold, But We Have Cheap Lobster

Maryland: If You Can Dream It, We Can Tax It

Massachusetts: Our Taxes Are Lower Than Sweden's (For Most Tax Brackets)

Michigan: First Line of Defense From The Canadians

Minnesota: 10,000 Lakes...And 10,000,000,000,000 Mosquitoes

Mississippi: Come And Feel Better About Your Own State

Missouri: Your Federal Flood Relief Tax Dollars At Work

Montana: Land Of The Big Sky, The Unabomber, Right-Wing Crazies, And Very Little Else

Nebraska: Ask About Our State Motto Contest

Nevada: Hookers and Poker!

New Hampshire: Go Away And Leave Us Alone

New Jersey: You Want A ##$%##! Motto? I Got Yer ##$%##! Motto Right Here!

New Mexico: Lizards Make Excellent pets

New York: You Have The Right To Remain Silent, You Have The Right To An Attorney...

North Carolina: Tobacco Is A Vegetable
North Dakota: We Really Are One of The Fifty States!
Ohio: At Least We're Not Michigan
Oklahoma: Like The Play, Only No Singing
Oregon: Spotted Owl…It's What's For Dinner
Pennsylvania: Cook With Coal
Rhode Island: We're Not really An Island
South Carolina: Remember The Civil War? We Didn't
 Actually Surrender
South Dakota: Closer Than North Dakota
Tennessee: The Educashun State
Texas: Si' Hablo Ing'les
Utah: Our Jesus Is Better Than Your Jesus
Vermont: Yep
Virginia: Who Says Government Stiffs And Slackjaw
 Yokels Don't Mix?
Washington: Help! We're Overrun By Nerds And Slackers!
Washington, D.C.: Wanna Be Mayor?
West Virginia: One Big Happy Family…Really!
Wisconsin: Come Cut The Cheese
Wyoming: Where Men Are Men…and the sheep are scared

———★———

Rumsfeld is giving a report to President Bush, "Three Brazilian soldiers were killed today in Iraq."

Bush says, "Oh, my God!" And he buries his head in his hands. The entire Cabinet is stunned. Usually George Bush shows no reaction whatsoever to these reports.

Just then, Bush looks up and says, "How many is a Brazilian?"

A demagogue is a politician who can rock the boat and persuade everyone else that they're in a terrible storm.

———★———

Political Philosophies Explained In Simple "Two Cow" Terms

Bureaucracy: You have two cows. The government takes them both, shoots one, milks the other, pays you for the milk, and then pours it down the drain.

Dictatorship: You have two cows. The government takes both, then shoots you.

Democracy: You have two cows. The government taxes you to the point that you must sell them both to support a man in a foreign country who has only one cow, which was a gift from your own government.

Corporate (including Educational Institutions): You have two cows. You lay one off; force the other to produce the milk of four cows, then act surprised when it drops dead.

A Christian Democrat: You have two cows. You keep one and give one to your neighbor.

An American Democrat: You have two cows. Your neighbor has none. You feel guilty for being successful. You vote people into office who tax your cows, forcing you to sell one to raise money to pay the tax. The people you voted for then take the tax money and buy a cow and give it to your neighbor. You feel righteous. Barbara Streisand sings for you.

A Fascist: You have two cows. The government seizes both and sells you the milk. You join the underground and start a campaign of sabotage. Capitalism, American Style: You have two cows. You sell one, buy a bull, and build a herd of cows. Republicanism: You have two cows. Your neighbor has none. So what?

Socialist: You have two cows. The government takes one and gives it to your neighbor. You form a cooperative to tell him how to manage his cow.

Communist: You have two cows. The government seizes both and provides you with milk. You wait in line for hours to get it. It is expensive and sour.

American Corporation: You have two cows. You sell one, lease it back to yourself and do an IPO on the second one. You force the two cows to produce the milk of four cows. You are surprised when one cow drops dead. You spin an announcement to the analysts stating you have downsized and are reducing expenses. Your stock goes up.

French Corporation: You have two cows. You go on strike because you want three cows. You go to lunch and drink wine. Life is good.

Japanese Corporation: You have two cows. You redesign them so they are one-tenth the size of an ordinary cow and produce twenty times the milk. They learn to travel on unbelievably crowded trains. Most are at the top of their class at cow school.

German Corporation: You have two cows. You engineer them so they are all blond, drink lots of beer, give excellent quality milk, and run a hundred miles an hour. Unfortunately they also demand thirteen weeks of vacation per year.

Italian Corporation: You have two cows but you don't know where they are. While ambling around, you see a beautiful woman. You break for lunch. Life is good.

Russian Corporation: You have two cows. You have some vodka. You count them and learn you have five cows. You have some more vodka. You count them again and learn you have forty-two cows. The Mafia shows up and takes over however many cows you really have.

Taliban Corporation: You have all the cows in Afghanistan, which are two. You don't milk them because you cannot touch any creature's private parts. You get a $40 million grant from the US government to find alternatives to milk production but use the money to buy weapons.

Iraqi Corporation: You have two cows. They go into hiding. They send radio tapes of their mooing.

Polish Corporation: You have two bulls. Employees are regularly maimed and killed attempting to milk them.

Belgian Corporation: You have one cow. The cow is schizophrenic. Sometimes the cow thinks he's French, other times he's Flemish. The Flemish cow won't share with the French cow. The French cow wants control of the Flemish cow's milk. The cow asks permission to be cut in half. The cow dies happy.

Florida Corporation: You have a black cow and a brown cow. Everyone votes for the best looking one. Some of the people who actually like the brown one best accidentally vote for the black one. Some people vote for both. Some people vote for neither. Some people can't figure out how to vote at all. Finally, a bunch of guys from out-of-state tell you which one you think is the best-looking cow.

California Corporation: You have millions of cows. They make real California cheese. Only five speak English. Most are illegals. Arnold likes the ones with the big udders.

———★———

A busload of politicians was driving down a country road when all of a sudden the bus ran off the road and crashed into a tree in an old farmer's field. After seeing what happened, he went over to investigate. He then proceeded to dig a hole and bury the politicians. When the local sheriff arrived, he saw the crashed bus and asked the old farmer where all the politicians had gone.

The old farmer said that he had buried them.

"Were they all dead?" the sheriff asked the farmer.

"Well, some of them said they weren't, but you know how those politicians lie."

———★———

What is the difference between the government and the Mafia?

One of them in organized.

An Israeli doctor says, "Medicine in my country is so advanced that we can take a kidney out of one man, put it in another, and have him looking for work in six weeks."

A German doctor says, "That is nothing, we can take a lung out of one person, put it in another, and have him looking for work in four weeks.

A Russian doctor says, "In my country, medicine is so advanced that we can take half a heart out of one person, put it in another, and have them both looking for work in two weeks."

The Texas doctor, not to be outdone, says, "You guys are way behind, we recently took a man with no brain out of Texas, put him in the White House for four years, and now half the country is looking for work."

———★———

Hillary Clinton goes to her doctor for a physical examination, only to find out that she's pregnant. She is furious—here she is in the middle of her first run for president, and as senator of New York this has happened to her.

She calls home, gets Bill on the phone, and immediately starts screaming. "How could you have let this happen? With all that's going on right now, you go and get me pregnant! How could you? I can't believe this! I just found out I am five weeks pregnant and it's all your fault! Your fault! Well, what have you got to say?"

There is nothing but dead silence on the phone.

She screams again, "Did you hear me?"

Finally she hears Bill's very, very quiet voice. In a barely audible whisper, "Who is this?"

———★———

George W. Bush is out jogging one morning, notices a little boy on the corner with a box. Curious, he runs over to the child and says, "What's in the box, kid?"

The little boy says, "Kittens, they're brand new kittens."

George W. laughs and says, "What kind of kittens are they?"

"Republicans," the child says.

"Oh, that's cute," George W. says, and he runs off.

A couple of days later George is running with his buddy Dick Cheney, and he spies the same boy with his box just ahead. George W. says to Dick, "You gotta check this out," and they both jog over to the boy with the box. George W. says, "Look in the box, Dick, isn't that cute? Look at those little kittens. Hey, kid, tell my friend Dick what kind of kittens they are."

The boy replies, "They're Democrats."

"Whoa!" George W. says, "I came by here the other day and you said they were Republicans. What's up?"

"Well," the kid says, "Their eyes are open now."

———★———

Airman Jones was assigned to the induction center where he advised new recruits about their government benefits, especially their GI Insurance. It wasn't long before Captain Smith noticed that Airman Jones was having a staggeringly high success rate selling insurance to nearly 100 percent of the recruits he advised. Rather than asking him about this, the captain stood at the back of the room and listened to Jones's sales pitch. Jones explained the basics of GI Insurance to the new recruits and then said, "If you are killed in a battle and have GI Insurance, the government has to pay $200,000 to your beneficiaries. But if you don't have GI Insurance and get killed in battle, the government only has to pay a maximum of $6,000."

"Now," he concluded, "which groups do you think they are going to send into battle first?"

——★——

The Republican National Convention is the presidential nominating convention of the Republican Party of the United States. The purpose of the Republican National Convention is to nominate an official candidate in an upcoming U.S. presidential election, and to adopt the party platform. This is a seriously funny look at their agenda:

Republican National Convention—Schedule of Events:

6:00 pm–Opening Prayer led by the Reverend Jerry Falwell

6:30 pm–Pledge of Allegiance

6:35 pm–Burning of Bill of Rights (excluding second amendment)

6:45 pm–Salute to the Coalition of the Willing

6:46 pm–Seminar Number One: "Getting your kid a military deferment"

7:30 pm–First Presidential Beer Bash for Bush

7:35 pm–Serve Freedom Fries

7:40 pm–EPA Address Number One: "Mercury: how to ignore the fourteen states Litigating against the U.S. government"

7:50 pm–William Safire on the dangers of non-Protestant religion

8:00 pm–Vote on which country to invade next

8:05 pm–Trent Lott recognizes/salutes the KKK contingent 08:10 pm–Call EMTs to revive Rush Limbaugh

8:15 pm–John Ashcroft Lecture: "The Homos are after your children"

8:30 pm–Roundtable discussion on reproductive rights (men only)

8:50 pm–Seminar Number Two: "Corporations: the government of the future"

9:00 pm–Condi Rice sings "Can't Help Lovin' Dat Man"

9:05 pm–Second Presidential Beer Bash for Bush

9:10 pm–EPA Address Number Two:" Trees: the real cause of forest fires"

9:15 pm–Roundtable discussion on the best way to bankrupt the Federal government.

9:30 pm–Break for secret meetings

9:35 pm–Dick Cheney on why we must invade Canada and find their weapons of mass destruction.

10:00 pm–Second prayer led by Pat Robertson

10:15 pm–Lecture by Karl Rove: "Doublespeak made easy"

10:30 pm–Rumsfeld demonstration of how to squint and talk macho

10:35 pm–Bush demonstration of his trademark "deer in the headlights" stare

10:40 pm–John Ashcroft demonstrates new mandatory kevlar chastity belt

10:45 pm–Clarence Thomas takes a minute to read the list of black Republicans

10:46 pm–Third Presidential Beer Bash for Bush

10:50 pm–Seminar Number Three: "Education: a drain on our nation's economy"

11:10 pm–Hillary Clinton Piñata

11:20 pm–Second Lecture by John Ashcroft: "Evolutionists—the dangerous new cult"

11:30 pm–Call EMTs to revive Rush Limbaugh again

11:35 pm–Blame Clinton

11:40 pm–Laura serves milk and cookies

11:45 pm–Pass the hat for the "Kenny Lay Defense Fund"

11:50 pm–Closing Prayer led by Jesus Himself

12:00 am–Nomination of George W. Bush as Holy Supreme Planetary Leader

—★—

Six former presidents are on a sinking boat:
Gerald Ford says: "What do we do?"
George W. Bush says: "Man the lifeboats!"
Ronald Reagan says: "What lifeboats?"
Jimmy Carter says: "Women first!"
Richard Nixon says: "Screw the women!"
Bill Clinton says: "You think we have time?"

—★—

Future historians will be able to study at the Jimmy Carter Library, the Gerald Ford Library, the Ronald Reagan Library, and the Bill Clinton Adult Bookstore.

—★—

The Center for Disease Control in Atlanta, Georgia, announced that former President Clinton has proven that you can get sex from aides.

Hillary Clinton goes to a fortuneteller who says, "Prepare to become a widow. Your husband will soon suffer a violent death."

Hillary takes a deep breath and asks, "Will I be acquitted?"

—★—

Only In America…

- Can a homeless combat veteran live in a cardboard box and a draft dodger live in the White House.

- Can a pizza get to your house faster than an ambulance.

- Are there handicapped parking spaces in front of a skating rink.

- Do drugstores make the sick walk all the way to the back of the store to get their prescriptions while healthy people can buy cigarettes at the front.

- Do people order a double cheeseburger, large fries, and a Diet Coke.

- Do banks leave both doors open and then chain the pens to the counters.

- Do we leave cars worth tens of thousands of dollars in the driveway and put our useless junk in the garage.

- Do we use answering machines to screen calls and then have call waiting so we won't miss a call from someone we didn't want to talk to in the first place.

- Do we use the word politics to describe the process so well: *poli* in latin means "many" and *tics* means "bloodsucking" creatures.

- Do they have drive-up ATM's with Braille lettering.

———★———

President Bush and Colin Powell are sitting in a bar. A guy recognizes them and walks over and says, "Wow, this is a real honor. What are you guys doing in here?"

Bush says, "We're planning WWIII. We're going to kill one hundred and forty million Iraqis and one blonde with big boobs."

"Why kill a blonde with big boobs?"

Bush turns to Powell, and says, "See smart ass, I told you no one would worry about the one hundred and forty million Iraqis!"

Politically Correct

Kentuckians, Tennesseans, and West Virginians will no longer be referred to as "Hillbillies." You must now refer to them as Appalachian-Americans.

———★———

The GOP National Committee announced today that it is changing the Republican emblem from an elephant to a condom because it more clearly reflects the party's political stance. A condom stands up to inflation, halts production, destroys the next generation, protects a bunch of pricks, and gives one a false sense of security while screwing others.

———★———

At a White House staff meeting there was a heated discussion about the health of Vice President Cheney and his angina problem. President Bush interrupted and stated emphatically that men do not have anginas. The president was especially perplexed when a staffer said that Cheney has acute angina.

———★———

In the beginning was the Plan.

And then came the Assumptions.

And the Assumptions were without form.

And the Plan was without substance.

And darkness was upon the face of the Workers.

And the Workers spoke among themselves saying, "This is a crock of s—t, and it stinks."

And the Workers went unto their Supervisors and said, "It is a pail of dung and we can't live with the smell."

And the Supervisors went unto their Managers, saying, "It is a container of excrement and is very strong, such that none may abide by it."

And the Managers went unto their Directors saying, "It is a vessel of fertilizer and none may abide its strength."

And the Directors spoke among themselves, saying, "It contains that which aids plant growth and is very strong."

And the Directors went to the Vice President, saying unto them, "It promotes growth and is very powerful."

"And the Vice President went to the President, saying unto him, "This new plan will actively promote growth and vigor of the company with very powerful effects."

And the President looked upon the Plan and saw that it was good. And the Plan became Policy. And that is how s—t happens.

——★——

General Norman Schwartzkopf was asked in an interview whether he thought there was room for forgiveness toward those who harbored and abetted the terrorists who perpetrated the 9/11 attacks:

"I believe forgiving them is God's function. Our job is simply to arrange the meeting."

The last four presidents are caught in a tornado and off they spin to Oz. They finally make it to the Emerald City and come before the Great Wizard.

"What brings you before the great Wizard of Oz?"

Jimmy Carter steps forward, "I've come for some courage."

Ronald Reagan steps forward, "Well, I think I need a brain!"

"Who comes next before the great and powerful Wizard of Oz?"

Up steps George Bush sadly, "I'm told by the American people that I need a heart."

"I've heard it's true. Consider it done."

There is a great silence. Bill Clinton is just standing there looking around, but not saying a word.

Irritated, the Wizard finally asks, "What do you want?"

"Is Dorothy here?"

———★———

Oxymorons:

Government Worker
Government Organization
Military Intelligence
Peace Force
Political Science
Sanitary Landfill

America Today:

If... a woman burns her thighs on the hot coffee she was holding in her lap while driving, she blames the restaurant.

your teen-ager goes ballistic and hurts himself, you blame the musician he listened to.

you smoke three packs a day for forty years and die of lung cancer your family blames the tobacco company.

your daughter gets pregnant by the captain of the football team you blame the school for poor sex education.

you crash your car into a tree while driving home drunk you blame the bartender.

your child gets an incurable disease because the needle he used to shoot heroin was dirty you blame the government for not providing clean ones.

your grandchildren are brats without manners you blame television.

a deranged madman shoots your friend you blame the gun manufacturer.

God Bless America, land of the free, home of the blame, where we can do whatever we want and give the blame to someone else.

George W. Bush was thrilled to be living in the White House, but something very strange happened on the very first night. He was awakened by George Washington's ghost.

"President Washington, what is the best thing I could do to help the country?"

"Set an honest and honorable example, just as I did," advised Washington.

Bush didn't sleep well and later that night the ghost of Thomas Jefferson moved through the dark bedroom. "Tom, what is the best thing I could do to help the country?"

"Cut taxes and reduce the size of the government," said Jefferson.

Bush still couldn't sleep and soon he saw another ghostly figure moving in the shadows. It was Abraham Lincoln's ghost. "Abe, what is the best thing I could do to help the country?"

"Go see a play!"

———★———

A cannibal was walking through the jungle and came upon a restaurant operated by a fellow cannibal.

Feeling somewhat hungry, he sat down and looked over the menu:

Broiled Missionary: $10.00
Fried Explorer: $15.00
Grilled Republican: $20.00
Baked Democrat: $1,000.00

The cannibal called the cook over and asked, "Why such a price difference for the Democrat?"

The cook replied, "Have you ever tried to clean one? They're so full of crap, it takes all morning to get them clean enough to cook."

———★———

Titanic versus Clinton

Titanic Video: $9.99 on the Internet
Clinton Video: $9.99 on the Internet
Titanic Video: Over three hours long
Clinton Video: Over three hours long
Titanic Video: The story of Jack and Rose, their forbidden love, and subsequent catastrophe
Clinton Video: The story of Bill and Monica, their forbidden love, and subsequent catastrophe
Titanic Video: In one part, Jack enjoys a good cigar
Clinton Video: Ditto for Bill
Titanic Video: Rose gets to keep her jewelry
Clinton Video: Monica is forced to return her gifts
Titanic Video: Rose remembers Jack for the rest of her life
Clinton Video: Monica doesn't remember jack
Titanic Video: Jack surrenders to an icy death
Clinton Video: Bill goes home to Hillary (basically the same thing)

Q: How can you tell that a politician is lying?
A: His lips are moving.

———★———

"If you consider that there was an average of 160,000 troops in Iraq during the first twenty-two months of the war, and a total of 2,112 deaths, that gives a firearm death rate of sixty per 100,000 soldiers.

The firearm death rate in Washington, D.C., was 80.6 per 100,000 for the same period. That means you were about 25 percent more likely to be shot and killed in the U.S. capital, which has some of the strictest gun control laws in the United States, than you were in Iraq.

Conclusion? "The United States should pull out of Washington."

———★———

A man goes to the White House and asks to see President Bush. The Marine on duty tells the guy that Bush isn't president anymore and to please leave. The man goes away.

The next day the man comes back to the White House and asks to see President Bush. The Marine on duty again tells him that Bush is not president anymore and to please go away. The man goes away.

The next day, he comes back again, and again the Marine is on duty.

The man asks to see President Bush, and the Marine, his patience worn out, says, "Why do you keep coming here asking for him? Bush is not president anymore!"

The man smiles and says, "I know, I just like hearing it."

———★——

As President Bush is getting off the helicopter in front of the White House, he has a baby pig under each arm. The Marine guard snaps to attention, salutes, and says: "Nice pigs, sir."

President Bush replies: "These are not pigs; these are authentic Texan Razorback Hogs. I got one for VP Cheney, and I got one for Defense Secretary Rumsfeld."

The Marine again snaps to attention, salutes, and replies, "Nice trade, sir."

———★——

An elderly man suffered a massive heart attack.

The family drove wildly to get him to the emergency room.

After what seemed like a very long wait, the E.R. doctor appeared, wearing his scrubs and a long face.

Sadly, he said, "I'm afraid he is brain-dead, but his heart is still beating."

"Oh, dear," cried his wife, her hands clasped against her cheeks with shock. "We've never had a Democrat in the family before!"

———★——

George W. was giving a speech in the Midwest. He praised the local community for the wonderful work they were doing and said what wonderful farmers he thought them to be.

Waving his arms in a grandiose gesture he said, "You see fields everywhere that have been plowed and planted. Very soon now, the forces of nature will cause the fields to produce a beautiful crop of corn, just one of nature's miracles."

A voice from the crowd replied, "It'd sure be a miracle, we planted wheat."

——★——

After his death, Osama bin Laden went to paradise.

He was greeted by George Washington, who slapped him across the face and yelled angrily, "How dare you attack the nation I helped conceive!"

Then Patrick Henry punched Osama in the nose, and James Madison kicked him in the groin.

Bin Laden was subjected to similar beatings from John Randolph, James Monroe, Thomas Jefferson, and sixty-six other early Americans.

As he writhed in pain on the ground, an angel appeared. Bin Laden groaned, "This is not what I was promised!"

The angel replied, "I told you there would be seventy-two Virginians waiting for you! What did you think I said?"

George Bush to George W: "Son, you are making the same mistake in Iraq that I made with your mother. I didn't pull out in time."

———★———

The real reason the United States invaded Iraq: George W. writes: To defeat terrorism we have no choice but to invade

~~Afriganist~~
~~Afgan~~
~~Aphghanis~~
~~Afgah~~
Iraq

———★———

"Well," the little old lady finally admitted to the persistent politician, "you're my second choice."

"I'm honored, ma'am," he gushed. "But may I ask, who's your first?"

"Oh," she said casually, "anybody else who's running."

———★———

After digging to a depth of 1,000 meters last year, Russian scientists found traces of copper wire dating back 1,000 years, and came to the conclusion that their ancestors already had a telephone network 1,000 years ago.

So, not to be outdone, in the weeks that followed, American scientists dug 2,000 meters and headlines in the U.S. papers read: "U.S. scientists have found traces of 2,000-year-old optical fibers, and have concluded that their ancestors already had advanced high-tech digital telephone 1,000 years earlier than the Russians."

One week later, the Israeli newspapers reported the following:

"After digging as deep as 5,000 meters, Israeli scientists have found absolutely nothing. They have concluded that 5,000 years ago, their ancestors were already using wireless technology."

———★———

A tired-looking reporter made his way out of the press conference that had been going on for over an hour. As he left the room, a woman stopped him.

"Who's speaking in there?" she asked.

"President Bush."

"About what?"

"He didn't say."

———★———

Resolving to surprise her husband, First Lady Hillary Clinton stopped by the Oval Office. She found Bill with his secretary sitting in his lap.

Without hesitating, he dictated, "and in conclusion, gentlemen, shortage or no shortage, I cannot continue to operate this office with just one chair."

The Difference Between Republicans And Democrats

A Republican and a Democrat were walking down the street when they came to a homeless person.

The Republican gave the homeless person his business card and told him come to his business for a job. He then took twenty dollars out of his pocket and gave it to the homeless person.

The Democrat was very impressed, and when they came to another homeless person, he decided to help. He walked over to the homeless person and gave him directions to the welfare office. He then reached into the Republican's pocket and gave him fifty dollars.

———★———

"Those who cast the votes decide nothing. Those who count the votes decide everything." –Joseph Stalin

———★———

Winston Churchill was once asked to name the chief qualification a politician should have.

His reply: "It's the ability to foretell what will happen tomorrow, next month, and next year and to explain afterward why it didn't happen."

A Brit, a Frenchman, and a Russian are viewing a painting of Adam and Eve frolicking in the Garden of Eden.

"Look at their reserve, their calm," mused the Brit. "They must be British."

"Nonsense," the Frenchman disagrees. "They're naked and so beautiful. Clearly they are French."

"No clothes, no shelter," the Russian points out, "they have only an apple to eat and they're being told this is paradise. Clearly they are Russian."

—★—

More Bumper Stickers We'd Like to See...

Don't Blame Me – I Voted For Gore...I Think

If God Meant for Us To Vote, He Would Have Given Us Candidates

What Popular Vote? I Voted – Didn't Matter

My Parents Retired to Florida & All I Got Was This Lousy President

Disney Gave Us Mickey. Florida Gave Us Dumbo

Who Is This Chad Guy & Why Is He Pregnant?

One Person, One Vote (May Not Apply In Certain States)

I Didn't Vote For His Daddy Either

Hillary and Chelsea are sitting around the table having a mother-daughter talk. Hillary says to Chelsea, "You have been going to college for a while now. Have you had sex yet?"

Chelsea says, "Well, not according to Dad."

———★———

While suturing up a cut on the hand of a seventy-five-year-old rancher whose hand had been caught in the gate while working his cattle, the doctor struck up a conversation with the old man. Eventually, the topic got around to Obama and his being our president.

The old rancher said, "Well, ya know, Obama is just a post turtle."

Now, not being familiar with the term, the doctor asked, "What's a post turtle?"

The old rancher said, "When you're driving down a country road and you come across a fence post with a turtle balanced on top, that's a post turtle."

The old rancher saw the puzzled look on the doctor's face so he continued to explain. "You know he didn't get up there by himself, he doesn't belong up there, he doesn't know what to do while he's up there, he sure as heck ain't goin' anywhere, and you just wonder what kind of dumb ass put him up there in the first place."

Once upon a time the government had a vast scrap yard in the middle of the desert. Congress said someone may steal from it at night so they created a night watchman position and hired a person for the job.

Then Congress thought, *how does the watchman do his job without instruction?* So they created a planning position and hired two people, one person to write the instructions and one person to do time studies. Then Congress thought, *how will we know the night watchman is doing the tasks correctly?*

So they created a quality control position and hired two people, one to do the studies and one to write the reports. Then Congress said, "How are these people going to get paid?" So they created the following positions—a time keeper and a payroll officer and hired two more people.

Then Congress thought, *who will be accountable for all of these people?* So they created an administrative position and hired three people—an administrative officer, an assistant administrative officer, and a legal secretary.

Then Congress said, "We have had this command in operation for one year and we are $280,000 over budget. We must cut back overall cost."

So they laid off the night watchman.

In a survey of American women, when asked, "Would you sleep with former President Bill Clinton?" 86 percent replied, "Not again."

———★———

Haircut at the mall: $10
Suit off the rack: $300

Losing the presidential election because 19,000 of your supporters are too damned stupid to follow the directions and fill out their ballots properly: priceless.

For everyone else, there's George W. Bush.

———★———

Bill Clinton and his driver were cruising along a country road one night when all of a sudden they hit a pig, killing it instantly. Bill told his driver to go up to the farmhouse and explain to the owners what had happened. About one hour later Bill sees his driver staggering back to the car with a bottle of wine in one hand, a cigar in the other, and his clothes all ripped and torn.

"What happened to you?" asked Bill.

"Well, the farmer gave me the wine, his wife gave me the cigar and his nineteen-year-old daughter made mad, passionate love to me," said the driver.

"My gosh, what did you tell them?" asks Clinton.

The driver replies, "I'm Bill Clinton's driver, and I just killed the pig."

The president wakes up one morning, looks out of the White House window, and sees "The President Sucks" written in the snow in urine. Furious, he calls in the FBI and demands the perpetrators be found.

Later that day the FBI agents return. "Well, sir," says the first agent, "the urine has been analyzed and it's the vice president's."

The president goes purple with rage and shouts, "Is that all?"

"Well, no, sir," says the agent, "it's the first lady's handwriting."

——★——

It isn't necessary for a politician to fool all the people all the time. A majority on Election Day is enough.

——★——

The candidate called his wife and said, "Congratulate me, I've just won the election!"

"Honestly, dear?"

"Now, why would you want to bring that up?"

——★——

Florida State Mottos:

- If you think we can't vote, wait 'till you see us drive.

- We count more than you do.

- If you don't like the way we count, then take I-95 and visit one of the other fifty-six states.

- We've been Gored by the bull of politics and we're Bushed.

- Relax, Retire, ReVote.

- What comes after 17,311?

- Where your vote counts and counts and counts.

- This is what you get for taking Elian away from us!

- We're number one! Wait! Recount!

———★———

Pick A Candidate

Candidate A: Associates with ward heelers and consults with astrologists. He's had two mistresses. He chain-smokes and drinks eight to ten martinis a day.

Candidate B: Was kicked out of office twice, sleeps until noon, used opium in college, and drinks a quart of brandy every evening.

Candidate C: Is a decorated war hero. He's a vegetarian, doesn't smoke, drinks an occasional beer, and hasn't had any illicit affairs.

Which of these candidates is your choice?
Candidate A is Franklin D. Roosevelt

Candidate B is Winston Churchill
Candidate C is Adolph Hitler
Scary, huh?

——★——

Palm Beach Pokey

(To the tune of "Hokey Pokey")

You put your stylus in,
You put your stylus out,
You put your stylus in,
And you punch Buchanan out.
You do the Palm Beach Pokey
And you turn the count around,
That's what it's all about!
You put the Gore votes in,
You put the Bush votes out,
You put the Gore votes in,
And you do another count.
You do the Palm Beach Pokey
And you turn the count around,
That's what it's all about!
You bring your lawyers in,
You drag the whole thing out,
You bring your lawyers in,
And you put it all in doubt.
You do the Palm Beach Pokey
And you turn the count around,
That's what it's all about!

You let your doctors spin,
You let the pundits spout,
You let your retirees sue,
And your people whine and pout.
You do the Palm Beach Pokey
And you turn the count around,
That's what it's all about!

———★———

'Twas The Week Past Election

'Twas a week past election and all through the land,
Not a president was chosen and no decision at hand.

The ballots were counted again and again In hopes that
Florida the vice president would win.

The governor had won it, or so he had said and thoughts
of his cabinet danced in his head. While Gore and his
lawyers and Bush and his too argued and argued about
what to do.

When down in Palm Beach arose such confusion, As
thousands of Democrats voted Buchanan! The box for
Buchanan was too close to Gore's, So Bush got the
most votes. Should Gore have had more?

Then what in the nation's eyes did appear?
But thousands of lawyers and lawsuits to hear.
Faster and faster the lawyers they came,

With a truckload of briefs, and people to blame.
And then the vice president said, and I quote: "We must hand count each Floridian's vote."
The country then watched as Florida reported
Numbers and figures the media distorted.

The vice president was weak, his chances were thin,
That in the end the presidency he'd win.

The governor's aides confidently touted
"We've won the election. Votes don't need to be counted."

No one cared anymore who was elected,
As long as it ended and one was selected.

As they pulled Palm Beach County and counted again,
America knew it never would end.
Thousands protested the votes that were tossed,
No one would ever concede he had lost.

And the media debated into the night,
Whether the holes should have been on the right.

And so no one knew from the west to the east,
Who got the most votes or who got the least?

But the voice of reason calmed everyone's fears: We'll do this again in another four years.

During his visit to the United States, the Pope met with the president. Instead of just an hour as scheduled, the meeting went on for two days. Finally, a weary president emerged to face the waiting news media. The president was smiling and announced the summit was a resounding success. He said he and the Pope agreed on 80 percent of the matters they discussed.

A few minutes later the Pope came out to make his statement. He looked tired and discouraged. Sadly, he announced his meeting with the president was a failure.

Incredulous, one reporter asked, "But your holiness, the president just announced the summit was a great success and the two of you agreed on eighty percent of the items discussed."

Exasperated, the Pope answered, "Yes, that's true, but we were talking about the Ten Commandments."

———★———

Wall Street is issuing three new bonds:
The Monica, which has no maturity.
The Gore, which has no interest, and
The Clinton, which has no principal.

———★———

Did you hear that Bill Clinton received a letter with anthrax in it? Don't worry. He didn't inhale.

After much arguing and deliberation historians this week have come up with a phrase to describe the Clinton Era.

It will be called: Sex between the Bushes.

———★———

The Canadian Government has decided to assist the United States in the war against terrorism. They have agreed to send us:

Two of their largest battleships, 6,000 ground troops, and six fighter jets.

After the exchange rate, the United States will receive:

One canoe, two mounties, and twelve flying squirrels.

———★———

The State of Texas, under the leadership of Governor George W. Bush was ranked:

Fiftieth in spending for teachers' salaries
Forty-ninth in spending on the environment
Forty-eighth in per-capita funding for public health
Forty-seventh in delivery of social services
Forty-second in child support collections
Forty-first in per-capita spending on public education

But, not all rankings were low. Bush did have Texas ranked:

Fifth in percentage of population living in poverty
First in air and water pollution

First in percentage of poor working parents without insurance
First in percentage of children without health insurance
First in executions (average every two weeks for Bush's five years)

It was said "Just think of what he could do for (to) the country if he were president."

——★——

A man plays hooky from work and goes golfing. On the second hole he notices a frog sitting in the fairway. As he is about to shoot he hears, "Ribbit nine iron." He hears it again and realizes it was the frog. He grabs his nine iron and hits the ball ten inches from the cup. He says, "Wow, that's amazing. You must be a lucky frog!"

The man takes the frog with him to the next hole. "Ribbit, three wood." The guy takes out his three wood and boom! Hole in one! By the end of the day he had played the best game in his life. The man decides to take this lucky frog to Vegas and at the casino asks the frog what to play. "Ribbit roulette. Ribbit three thousand dollars, black six." He figures this is a million-to-one shot, but after his lucky golf game he goes for it.

Boom! Tons of cash comes sliding across the table. The man takes his winnings and buys the best room in the hotel. He sits down and says, "Frog, I don't know how to repay you. You've won me all this money, and I will be forever grateful."

The frog replies, "Ribbit kiss me." He figures why not, after all the frog did for him, he deserves it. With a kiss the frog turns into a gorgeous twenty-one-year-old girl. "And that your honor is how the girl ended up in my room. So help me God or my name is not William Jefferson Clinton."

———★———

The Situation: You are in Texas covering a flood that has wiped out towns and made thousands homeless. You are traveling alone, looking for a shot to convey the enormity of the tragedy. You come across George W. Bush, whom the floodwaters have swept from his four-by-four. He is clinging to a tree limb, but is clearly losing his grip and is about to go under. You can either put down your camera and save him or take what will no doubt be a Pulitzer Prize winning shot of him as the torrent carries him away.

So here's the question: which lens would you use?

———★———

Health care costs are rising uncontrollably across the world. In America, taxes have been on the rise just to pay for them.

In England, they have begun rationing health care services and in some cases they have waiting lists for services just to reduce costs even more. In fact, they now have a nine-month waiting list for abortions.

A visitor from Holland was chatting with his American friend and was jokingly explaining about the red, white, and blue in the Netherlands' flag. "Our flag symbolizes our taxes," he said. "We get red when we talk about them, white when we get our tax bill, and blue after we pay them."

"That's the same with us," the American said, "only we see stars, too."

———★———

The Thinnest Books

How To Land A Plane At Martha's Vineyard by JFK, Jr.

The Wild Years by Al Gore

The Book of Virtues by Bill Clinton

———★———

Lots of folks are forced to skimp to support a government that won't.

Q: How is Bin Laden like Fred Flintstone?
A: Both look out their windows and see Rubble.

Q: What do Bin Laden and Hiroshima have in common?
A: Nothing yet.

——★——

Democrats Versus Republicans

Democrats buy most of the books that have been banned somewhere.

Republicans form censorship committees and read them as a group.

Democrats give their worn-out clothes to those less fortunate.

Republicans wear theirs.

Republicans employ exterminators.

Democrats step on the bugs.

Democrats name their children after currently popular sports figures, politicians, and entertainers.

Republican children are named after their parents or grandparents, according to where the money is.

Democrats keep trying to cut down on smoking but are not successful.

Neither are Republicans.

Republicans tend to keep their shades drawn, although there is seldom any reason why they should.

Democrats ought to but don't.

Republicans study the financial pages of the newspaper.

Democrats put them in the bottom of the birdcage.

Republicans raise dahlias, Dalmatians, and eyebrows.

Democrats raise Airedales, kids, and taxes.

Democrats eat the fish they catch.

Republicans hang them on the wall.

Republican boys date Democratic girls. They plan to marry Republican girls, but feel that they're entitled to a little fun first.

Democrats make plans and then do something else. Republicans follow the plans their grandfathers made.

Republicans sleep in twin beds—some even in separate rooms.

That is why there are more Democrats.

——★——

The Americans and Russians at the height of the arm's race realized that if they continued in the usual manner they were going to blow up the whole world. One day, they sat down and decided to settle the whole dispute with one dogfight. They would have five years to breed the best fighting dog in the world and whichever side's dog won would be entitled to dominate the world. The losing side would have to lay down its arms.

The Russians found the biggest, meanest Doberman and Rottweiler bitches in the world and bred them with the biggest, meanest Siberian wolves. They selected only the biggest and strongest puppy from each litter, removed his siblings, which gave him all the milk. They used steroids and trainers and after five years came up with the biggest meanest dog the world had ever seen. Its cage needed steel bars that were five inches thick and nobody could get near it.

When the day came for the dogfight, the Americans showed up with a strange animal. It was a nine-foot long Dachshund. Everyone felt sorry for the Americans because they knew there was no way that this dog could possibly last ten seconds with the Russian dog. When the cages were opened up, the Dachshund came out of its cage and slowly waddled over toward the Russian dog. The Russian dog snarled and leaped out of its cage and charged the American Dachshund. But, when it got close enough to bite the Dachshund's neck, the Dachshund opened its mouth and consumed the Russian dog in one bite. There was nothing left of the Russian dog.

The Russians came up to the Americans, shaking their heads in disbelief.

"We don't understand how this could have happened. We had our best people working for five years with the meanest Doberman and Rottweiler bitches in the world and the biggest, meanest Siberian wolves."

"That's nothing," an American replied. "We had our best plastic surgeons working for five years to make an alligator look like a Dachshund."

Can you imagine working for a company that has a little more than 500 employees and has the following statistics:

Twenty-nine have been accused of spousal abuse

Seven have been arrested for fraud

Nineteen have been accused of writing bad checks

One hundred and seventeen have directly or indirectly bankrupted at least two businesses

Three have done time for assault

Seventy-one cannot get a credit card due to bad credit

Fourteen have been arrested on drug-related charges

Eight have been arrested for shoplifting

Twenty-one are currently defendants in lawsuits

Eighty-four have been arrested for drunk driving in the last year

Can you guess which organization this is?

It's the 535 members of the United States Congress. The same group that cranks out hundreds of new laws each year designed to keep the rest of us in line.

——★——

President George Bush made an official announcement today regarding his plans when Gulf War II is over.

First on the list was the division of Iraq into three provinces:

Leaded, Unleaded and Diesel.

George W. Bush ran into Colin Powell's office exclaiming, "Dick Cheney hanged himself in his bathroom!"

Colin Powell says, "Oh, no! Did you cut him down?"

"Cut him down? How could I cut him down? He wasn't dead yet!"

——★——

A big earthquake with the strength of 8.1 on the Richter scale has hit Mexico. Two million Mexicans have died and over a million are injured. The country is totally ruined, and the government doesn't know where to start with asking for help to rebuild.

The rest of the world is in shock. Canada is sending troopers to help the Mexican army control the riots. Saudi Arabia is sending oil. Other Latin American countries are sending supplies. The European community (except France) is sending food and money. The United States, not to be outdone, is sending four million replacement Mexicans.

——★——

George W. Bush went to see the doctor to get the results of his brain scan. The doctor said: "Mr. President, I have some bad news for you. First, we have discovered that your brain has two sides: the left side and the right side."

Bush interrupted, "Well, that's normal, isn't it? I thought everybody had two sides to their brain?"

The doctor replied, "That's true, Mr. President. But your brain is very unusual because on the left side there isn't anything right, while on the right side there isn't anything left."

Memo (after 9/11)

To: Al Gore
Re: Election Results

Dear Al:
We found some more votes. You won. When do you want to take over?

Sincerely,
George W. Bush

———★———

George Dubya and Dick Cheney are watching the six o'clock news one evening. Cheney bets Dubya $50 that the man in the lead story, who is threatening to jump from a forty-story building, will jump. "I'll take that bet," Dubya replied.

A few minutes later, the newscaster breaks in to report that the man had, indeed, jumped from the building. Cheney, feeling sudden guilt for having bet on such an incident, turns to Dubya and tells him that he does not need to pay the $50.

"No, a bet's a bet," Dubya replied, "I owe you fifty dollars."

Cheney, feeling even guiltier, replied, "No, you don't understand, I saw the three o'clock edition, so I knew how it was going to turn out."

"That's okay," said Dubya, "I saw it earlier, too, but I didn't think he'd do it again."

Bush's Psalm

"Bush is my shepherd, I shall be in want. He leadeth me beside the still factories, He maketh me to lie down on park benches, He restoreth my doubts about the Republican Party, He guideth me onto the paths of unemployment for the party's sake. I do fear the evildoers, for thou talkst about them constantly. Thy tax cuts for the rich and thy deficit spending they do discomfort me. Thou anointeth me with never-ending debt, And my savings and assets shall soon be gone. Surely poverty and hard living shall follow me, And my jobless children shall dwell in my basement forever."

—★—

A squad of American soldiers was patrolling along the Iraqi border when they came upon the badly mangled body of an Iraqi soldier in a ditch at the side of the road. A short distance up the road they found a badly mangled American soldier in a ditch on the other side of the road that was still barely alive. They knelt beside him, cradled his blood-covered head and asked him what had happened.

"Well," he whispered, "I was walking down this road armed to the teeth when I came across this heavily armed Iraqi border guard. I looked him right in the eye and shouted, "Saddam Hussein is an unprincipled, lying jerk!"

He looked me right in the eye and shouted back, "George W. Bush is an unprincipled, lying jerk! We were standing there shaking hands when the truck hit us."

This morning, from a cave somewhere in Pakistan, Taliban Minister of Migration, Mohammed Omar, warned the United States and Canada that if military action against Iraq continues, Taliban authorities will cut off America's and Canada's supply of convenience store managers.

And if this action does not yield sufficient results, cab drivers will be next, followed by Dell and Sprint customer service reps. It's getting ugly.

———★———

Latest Science Discovery

The densest element yet known to science has been discovered. The new element has been named "Bushcronium."

Bushcronium has one neutron, twelve assistant neutrons, seventy-five deputy neutrons, and 224 assistant deputy neutrons, giving it an atomic mass of 911.

These particles are held together by dark forces called morons, which are surrounded by vast quantities of lepton-like particles called peons.

The symbol for Bushcronium is "W."

Bushcronium's mass actually increases over time, as these morons randomly interact with various elements in the atmosphere and become assistant deputy neutrons in a Bushcronium molecule, forming a large cluster of idiotopes.

This characteristic of moron-promotion leads some scientists to believe that Bushcronium is formed whenever morons reach a critical mass also known as "Critical Morass."

When catalyzed with money, Bushcronium activates Foxnewsium, an element radiating several orders of magnitude more energy, mostly as incoherent noise, since it has half as many peons but twice as many morons. Isn't science wonderful?

———★———

A first grade teacher explains to her class that she is a liberal Democrat. She asks her students to raise their hands if they were liberal Democrats, too. Not really knowing what a liberal Democrat was, but wanting to be like their teacher, their hands flew up into the air. There was, however, one exception. A girl named Lucy had not gone along with the crowd. The teacher asks her why she has decided to be different.

"Because I'm not a liberal Democrat."

"Then, what are you?"

"Why I'm a proud conservative Republican," boasts the little girl.

The teacher, a little perturbed and her face slightly red, asked Lucy why she is a conservative Republican.

"Well, I was brought up to trust in myself instead of relying on an intrusive government to care for me and do all of my thinking. My dad and mom are conservative Republicans, and I am a conservative Republican, too."

The teacher, now angry, loudly says, "That's no reason! What if your mom was a moron, and your dad was a moron. What would you be then?

She paused and let out a smile. "Then I'd be a liberal Democrat."

———★———

Battle Hymn of The Republicans

(to the tune of the "Battle Hymn of the Republic")
Mine eyes have seen the bungling of that stumbling
    moron Bush;
He has blathered all the drivel that the neo-cons
    can push;
He has lost sight of all reason 'cause his head is up
    his tush;
The Doofus marches on.
I have heard him butcher syntax like a kindergar-
    ten fool;
There is warranted suspicion that he never went
    to school;
Should we fault him for the policies — or is he just
    their tool?
The lies keep piling on.
Glory! Glory! How he'll Screw Ya'!
Glory! Glory! How he'll Screw Ya'!
Glory! Glory! How he'll Screw Ya'!
His wreckage will live on.

I have seen him cut the taxes of the billionaires' lone heir;
As he spends another zillion on an aircraft carrier;
Let the smokestacks keep polluting — do we really
    need clean air?The surplus is now gone.
Glory! Glory! How he'll Screw Ya'!
Glory! Glory! How he'll Screw Ya'!
Glory! Glory! How he'll Screw Ya'!
Your safety net is gone!
Now he's got a mighty hankerin' to bomb a pros-
    trate state;
Though the whole world knows its crazy — and the
    U.N. says to wait;
When he doesn't have the evidence, "We
    must prevaricate."
Diplomacy is done!
Oh, a trumped-up war is excellent; we have no
    moral bounds;
Should the reasons be disputed, we'll just make up
    other grounds;
Enraging several billions — to his brainless-
    ness redounds;
The Doofus marches on!
Glory! Glory! How he'll Screw Ya'!
Glory! Glory! How he'll Screw Ya'!
Glory! Glory! How he'll Screw Ya'!
THIS...DOO...FUS...MAR...CHES...ON

Sandy Rozelman

New Sexually Transmitted Disease Warning

Worse than SARS and Bird Flu combined, The Center for Disease Control has issued a warning about a new virulent strain of Sexually Transmitted Disease. The disease is contracted through dangerous and high-risk behavior. The disease is called Gonorrhea Lectim and pronounced "gonna re-elect him." Many victims contracted it in 2004, after having been screwed for the past four years. Cognitive characteristics of individuals infected include: anti-social personality disorders, delusions of grandeur with messianic overtones, extreme cognitive dissonance, inability to incorporate new information, pronounced xenophobia and paranoia, inability to accept responsibility for own actions, cowardice masked by misplaced bravado, uncontrolled facial smirking, ignorance of geography and history, tendencies toward evangelical theocracy, categorical all-or-nothing behavior. Naturalists and epidemiologists are amazed at how this destructive disease originated only a few years ago from a bush found in Texas.

———★———

The Los Angeles Police Department, the FBI, and the CIA are all trying to prove that they are the best at apprehending criminals. The president decides to give them a test. He releases a rabbit into a forest and each of them has to catch it.

The CIA goes in. They place animal informants throughout the forest. They question all plant and mineral witnesses. After three months of extensive investigation, they conclude that rabbits do not exist.

The FBI goes in. After two weeks with no leads, they burn the forest, killing everything in it—including the rabbit—and make no apologies. Their press release on their "successful operation" notes "The rabbit had it coming."

The LAPD goes in. They come out two hours later with a badly beaten bear. The bear is yelling, "Okay, okay, I'm a rabbit, I'm a rabbit!"

———★———

Bill Clinton started jogging near his new home in Chappaqua. But on each run he happened to jog past a hooker standing on the same street corner, day after day. With some apprehension he would brace himself as he approached her for was most certainly to follow.

"Fifty dollars!" she would cry out from the curb.

"No, five dollars!" fired back Clinton. This ritual between Bill and the hooker continued for days. He'd run by and she'd yell, "Fifty dollars!" And he'd yell back, "Five dollars!"

One day however, Hillary decided that she wanted to accompany her husband on his jog! As the jogging couple neared the problematic street corner, Bill realized the "pro" would bark her fifty-dollar offer and Hillary would wonder what he'd really been doing on his past outings.

As they jogged into the turn that would take them past the corner, Bill became even more apprehensive than usual. Sure enough, there was the hooker! Bill tried to avoid the prostitute's eyes as she watched the pair jog past. Then, from the sidewalk, the hooker yelled, "See what you get for five bucks?"

———★———

Why Did The Chicken Cross The Road?

Barack Obama: The chicken crossed the road because it was time for a change! The chicken wanted change!

John McCain: My friends, that chicken crossed the road because he recognized the need to engage in cooperation and dialogue with all the chickens on the other side of the road.

Sarah Palin: Because, praise Jesus, I was gonna shoot his sorry liberal ass for blocking my view of Russia!

George W. Bush: "We don't really care why the chicken crossed the road. We just want to know if the chicken is on our side of the road or not. The chicken is either against us or for us. There is no middle ground here. I don't believe we need to get the chickens across the road. I say give the road to the chickens and let them decide.

Dick Cheney: Chickens are big-time because they have wings. They could fly if they wanted to. Chickens don't want to cross the road. They don't need help crossing the road. In fact, I'm not interested in crossing the road myself. Where's my gun?

Hillary Clinton: I have vast experience with chickens and if elected, I will ensure that *every* chicken has the ability to cross any road they desire. When I was First Lady, I personally helped that little chicken to cross the road. This experience makes me uniquely qualified to ensure, right from day one, that every chicken in this country gets the chance it deserves to cross the road. But then, this really isn't about me…

Bill Clinton: I did not cross the road with *that* chicken! What do you mean by chicken? Could you define chicken please? What is your definition of chicken?

Al Gore: I invented the chicken! I fight for the chickens, and I am fighting for the chickens right now. I will not give up on the chickens crossing the road. I will fight for the chickens, and I will not disappoint them.

Joe Lieberman: I believe that every chicken has the right to worship his or her God in his or her own way. Crossing the road is a spiritual journey and no chicken should be denied the right to cross the road in his or her own way.

Colin Powell: Now to the left of the screen, you can clearly see the satellite image of the chicken crossing the road…

Ralph Nader: Chickens are misled into believing there is a road by the evil tire makers. Chickens aren't ignorant, but our society pays tire makers to create the need for these roads and then lures chickens into believing there is an advantage to crossing them. Down with the roads; up with chickens.

John Kerry: Although I voted to let the chicken cross the road, I am now against it! It was the wrong road to cross, and I was misled about the chicken's intentions. I am not for it now and will remain against it.

Richard M. Nixon: The chicken did not cross the road. I repeat: the chicken did not cross the road. I do not know any chickens. I have never known any chickens.

Saddam Hussein: This was an unprovoked act of rebellion, and we were quite justified in dropping fifty tons of nerve gas on it.

Ronald Reagan: What chicken?

L.A. Police Department: Give us five minutes with the chicken and we'll find out.

Karl Marx: It was historically inevitable.

Colonel Sanders: Did I miss one?

—★—

The Democratic Party has a crisis of monumental proportions. They don't know whether to vote for the "Nut" with two boobs or the "Boob" with two nuts.

Everyone wonders why Muslim terrorists are so quick to commit suicide. Let's see now:

No beer, no bars, no radio, no television, no Playboy or penthouse.

No rugby, no football, no basketball, no baseball, no golf. no dancing, no music.

No bikinis, no nude beaches, no summer mini skirts and braless beauties, no pork, no ham, no bacon, no hot dogs, no burgers, no lobster, no shellfish. No Christmas.

Rags for clothes and dishtowels for hats.

Constant wailing from the guy next door because he's sick and there are no doctors.

You can't shave. Your wife can't shave. You can't even shave your wife.

Sand is everywhere. Sand gets into everything.

You wipe your backside with your left hand without toilet paper, and if they catch you stealing, they chop off your good hand and you must eat with your dirty hand.

You can't shower to wash off the smell of donkey cooked over burning camel dung.

The women have to wear baggy dresses and veils at all times. Your bride is picked by someone else. She smells just like your camel, but your camel has a better disposition.

Then your leaders tell you that when you die, you get seventy-two virgins and it all gets better!

So…nope…no mystery here! And for those virgins, heaven isn't quite what they expected.

A Somalian arrives in Minneapolis as a new immigrant to the United States. He stops the first person he sees walking down the street and says, "Thank you Mr. American for letting me in this country, giving me housing, food stamps, free medical care, and free education!"

The passerby says, "You are mistaken, I am Mexican."

The man goes on and encounters another passerby. "Thank you for having such a beautiful country here in America!"

The person says, "I not American, I Vietnamese."

The new arrival walks further, and the next person he sees he stops, shakes his hand, and says, "Thank you for the wonderful America!"

That person puts up his hand and says, "I am from Middle East. I am not American!"

He finally sees a nice lady and asks, "Are you an American?"

She says, "No, I am from Africa!"

Puzzled, he asks her, "Where are all the Americans?"

The African lady checks her watch and says, "Probably at work."

———★———

Do you know what happened this week back in 1850,
    162 years ago?
California became a state,
The state had no electricity.
The state had no money.
Almost everyone spoke Spanish
There were gunfights in the streets.

So basically, it was just like California is today,
Except the women had real breasts,
And the men didn't hold hands.

———★———

Are you a Democrat, a Republican, or a redneck? Here is a little test that will help you decide. The answer can be found by posing the following question:

You're walking down a deserted street with your wife and two small children. Suddenly, an Islamic terrorist with a huge knife comes around the corner, locks eyes with you, screams obscenities, praises Allah, raises the knife, and charges at you. You are carrying a Kimber 1911 cal. 45 ACP, and you are an expert shot. You have mere seconds before he reaches you and your family. What do you do?

Democrat's Answer:

Well, that's not enough information to answer the question!

Does the man look poor or oppressed?

Have I ever done anything to him that would inspire him to attack?

Could we run away? What does my wife think? What about the kids?

Could I possibly swing the gun like a club and knock the knife out of his hand?

What does the law say about this situation?

Does the pistol have appropriate safety built into it?

Why am I carrying a loaded gun anyway, and what kind of message does this send to society and to my children?

Is it possible he'd be happy with just killing me?

Does he definitely want to kill me, or would he be content just to wound me?

If I were to grab his knees and hold on, could my family get away while he was stabbing me? Should I call 9-1-1?

Why is this street so deserted? We need to raise taxes, have paint and weed day and make this a happier, healthier street that would discourage such behavior.

This is all so confusing! I need to debate this with some friends for few days and try to come to a consensus.

Republican's Answer: Bang!

Redneck's Answer: Bang! Bang! Bang! Bang! Bang! Bang! Bang! Bang! Bang! Click... (sounds of reloading) Bang! Bang! Bang! Bang! Bang! Bang! Bang! Bang! Bang! Click

Daughter: "Nice grouping, Daddy! Were those the Winchester Silver Tips or Hollow Points?"

Son: "Can I shoot the next one?"

Wife: "You ain't taking that to the taxidermist!"

———★———

There will be no nativity scene in the United States Congress this year! The Supreme Court has ruled that there cannot be a nativity scene in the United States' capital this Christmas season. This isn't for any religious reason; they simply have not been able to find three wise men and a virgin in the nation's capitol.

There was no problem, however, finding enough asses to fill the stable.

Hillary Clinton, the lead presidential Democrat Party candidate, is for banning all guns in America. She is considered by those who have dealt with her as more than just a little self-righteous.

At a recent rural elementary school meeting in North Florida, she asked the kids and the audience for total quiet. Then, in the silence, she started to slowly clap her hands, once every few seconds. Holding the audience in total silence, she said, "Every time I clap my hands, a child in America dies from gun violence."

A young voice with a proud southern accent from the front of the crowd pierced the quiet: "Well then, would you please stop clapping!"

Did you ever notice: When you put the two words *the* and *IRS* together it spells "theirs"?

———★———

America is the land of opportunity. Everybody can become a taxpayer. The trick is to stop thinking of it as "your" money.
    Signed, The IRS

———★———

People who complain about taxes can be divided into two classes: men and women.

———★———

Isn't it appropriate that the month of the tax begins with April Fool's Day and ends with cries of "May Day"?

———★———

We've got what it takes to take what you've got.– The IRS.

———★———

I believe we should all pay our tax bill with a smile. I tried but they wanted cash.

Computer Viruses

The George W. Bush Virus–Causes your computer to keep looking for viruses of mass destruction.

The John Kerry Virus–Stores data on both sides of the disk and causes little purple hearts to appear on screen.

The Clinton Virus–Gives you a permanent hard drive; with no memory

The Al Gore Virus–Causes your computer to keep counting and re-counting

The Bob Dole Virus–Makes a new hard drive out of an old floppy

The Lewinsky Virus–Sucks all the memory out of your computer, and then e-mails everyone about what it did

The Arnold Schwarzenegger Virus–Terminates some files, leaves, but will be back

The Mike Tyson Virus–Quits after two bytes

The Oprah Winfrey Virus–Your 200 GB hard drive shrinks to 100 GB, and then slowly expands to re-stabilize around 350 GB

The Ellen Degeneres Virus–Hard disks can no longer be inserted

The Prozac Virus–Totally screws up your RAM, but your processor doesn't care!

The Michael Jackson Virus–Only attacks minor files

The Lorena Bobbitt Virus–Reformats your hard drive into a 3.5-inch floppy...then discards it through Windows

Benjamin Franklin said nothing is certain but death and taxes: but death isn't annual.

——★——

Taxation with representation ain't so hot either.

——★——

Marketing 101:
Things you might want to know

The buzzword in today's business world is *marketing*. However, people often ask for a simple explanation of marketing. Well, here it is:

You're a woman and you see a handsome guy at a party. You go up to him and say, "I'm fantastic in bed." That's direct marketing.

You're at a party with a bunch of friends and see a handsome guy. One of your friends goes up to him and, pointing at you, says, "She's fantastic in bed." That's advertising.

You see a handsome guy at a party. You go up to him and get his telephone number. The next day you call and say, "Hi, I'm fantastic in bed." That's telemarketing.

You see a guy at a party; you straighten your dress. You walk up to him and pour him a drink. You say, "May I?" and reach up to straighten his tie, brushing your breast lightly against his arm, and then say, "By the way, I'm fantastic in bed." That's public relations.

You're at a party and see a handsome guy. He walks up to you and says, "I hear you're fantastic in bed." That's brand recognition.

You're at a party and see a handsome guy. He fancies you, but you talk him into going home with your friend. That's a sales rep.

Your friend can't satisfy him so he calls you. That's tech support.

You're on your way to a party when you realize that there could be handsome men in all these houses you're passing. So you climb onto the roof of one situated toward the center and shout at the top of your lungs, "I'm fantastic in bed!" That's junk mail.

You are at a party and this well-built man walks up to you and grabs your ass. That's the former governor of Arkansas.

You like it, but twenty years later your attorney decides that you were offended. That's America.

———★———

An attorney arrived home late after a very tough day trying to get a stay of execution for a client who was due to be hanged for murder at midnight. His last-minute plea for clemency to the governor had failed, and he was feeling worn out and de-pressed. As soon as he walked through the door at home, his wife started on him about, "What time of night to be getting home is this? Where have you been? Dinner is cold, and I'm not reheating it." And on and on and on.

Too shattered to play his usual role in this familiar ritual, he poured himself a shot of whiskey and headed off for a long, hot soak in the bathtub, pursued by the predictable sarcastic remarks as he dragged himself up the stairs. While he was in the bath, the phone rang. The wife answered and was told that her husband's client, John Wright, had been granted a stay of execution after all. Wright would not be hanged tonight.

Finally realizing what a terrible day he must have had, she decided to go upstairs and give him the good news. As she opened the bathroom door, she was greeted by the sight of her husband, bent over naked, drying his legs and feet. "They're not hanging Wright tonight," she said, to which he whirled around and screamed:

"For the love of God, woman, don't you ever stop?"

———★———

Democrats are sexy…whoever heard of a nice piece of elephant?

———★———

If we quit voting…will they all go away?

———★———

An older couple had a son, who was still living with his parents. The parents were a little worried, as the son was still unable to decide about his career path…so they decided to do a small test.

They took a ten-dollar bill, a Bible, and a bottle of whiskey and put them on the front hall table. Then they hid, hoping he would think they weren't at home.

The father told the mother, "If he takes the money he will be a businessman, if he takes the Bible he will be a priest, but if he takes the bottle of whiskey, I'm afraid our son will be a drunkard."

So the parents took their place in the nearby closet and waited nervously. Peeping through the keyhole they saw their son arrive home. He saw the note they had left, saying they'd be home later. Then, he took the ten-dollar bill, looked at it against the light, and slid it in his pocket. Then he took the Bible, flicked through it, and took it also.

Finally, he grabbed the bottle, opened it, and took an appreciative whiff to be assured of the quality. Then he left for his room, carrying all the three items.

The father slapped his forehead and said: "Darn, it's even worse than I ever imagined…"

"What do you mean?" his wife inquired.

"Our son is going to be a politician!" replied the concerned father.

—★—

St. Peter was at the pearly gates checking up on the people waiting to enter heaven. He asked the next one in line, "So, who are you, and what did you do on Earth?"

The fellow said, "I'm Barack Hussein Obama, and I was the first black to be elected president of the United States."

St. Peter said, "The US? A black president? You gotta be kidding me! When did this happen?"

Obama said, "Yesterday."

The Irish can't figure out why people are even bothering to hold an election in the United States.

On one side, you have a bitch who is a lawyer, married to a lawyer, running against a lawyer who is married to a bitch who is a lawyer.

On the other side, you have a war hero married to a good-looking woman who owns a beer distributorship.

What are you lads thinking over there?

———★———

The Ant and the Grasshopper

Old version: The ant works hard in the withering heat all summer long, building his house and laying up supplies for the winter. The grasshopper thinks the ant is a fool and laughs and dances and plays the summer away. Come winter, the ant is warm and well fed. The grasshopper has no food or shelter, so he dies out in the cold.

Moral of the story: Be responsible for yourself!

Modern version: The ant works hard in the withering heat all summer long, building his house and laying up supplies for the winter. The grasshopper thinks the ant is a fool and laughs and dances and plays the summer away. Come winter, the shivering grasshopper calls a press conference and demands to know why the ant should be allowed to be warm and well fed while others are cold and starving.

CBS, NBC, PBS, CNN, and ABC show up to provide pictures of the shivering grasshopper next to a video of the ant in his comfortable home with a table filled with food. America is stunned by the sharp contrast. How can this be, that in a country of such wealth, this poor grasshopper is allowed to suffer so?

Kermit the Frog appears on Oprah with the grasshopper and everyone cries when they sing "It's Not Easy Being Green."

Jesse Jackson stages a demonstration in front of the ant's house where the news stations film the group singing "We Shall Overcome." Jesse then has the group kneel down to pray to God for the grasshopper's sake.

Nancy Pelosi and John Kerry exclaim in an interview with Larry King that the ant has gotten rich off the back of the grasshopper and both call for an immediate tax hike on the ant to make him pay his fair share.

Barack Obama gives an eloquent speech on the down trodden and the government's responsibility to them.

Finally, the EEOC drafts the Economic Equity and Anti-Grasshopper Act retroactive to the beginning of the summer. The ant is fined for failing to hire a proportionate number of green bugs and, having nothing left to pay his retroactive taxes, his home is confiscated by the government.

Hillary gets her old law firm to represent the grasshopper in a defamation suit against the ant, and the case is tried before a panel of federal judges that Bill Clinton appointed from a list of single-parent welfare recipients.

The ant loses the case.

The story ends as we see the grasshopper finishing up the last bites of the ant's food while the government house he is in, which just happens to be the ant's old house, crumbles around him because he doesn't maintain it.

The ant has disappeared in the snow.

The grasshopper is found dead in a drug related incident and the house, now abandoned, is taken over by a gang of spiders who terrorize the once peaceful neighborhood.

Moral of the story: Be careful how you vote in 2008.

———★———

Try this at your job and tell me how it works out:

Dear Boss,

I have enjoyed working here these past several years. You have paid me very well, given me benefits beyond belief. I have three to four months off per year and a pension plan that will pay my salary 'till the day I die and a health plan that most people can only dream about.

Despite this I plan to take the next twelve to eighteen months to find a new position.

During this time I will show up for work when it is convenient. In addition, I fully expect to draw my full salary and all the other perks associated with my current job.

Oh, yes, if my search for this new job proves fruitless, I will be back with no loss in pay or status. Before you say anything, remember that you have no choice in the matter. I can and will do this.

Sincerely,

Every senator or congressman running for president.

———★———

Two Middle East mothers are sitting in a cafe chatting over a plate of tabouli and a pint of goat's milk. The older of the mothers pulls a bag out of her purse and starts flipping through photos. And they start reminiscing.

"This is my oldest son, Mohammed. He would be twenty-four years old now."

"Yes, I remember him as a baby," says the other mother cheerfully.

"He's a martyr now though," mum confides.

"Oh, so sad, dear," says the other.

"And this is my second son, Kalid. He would be twenty-one."

"Oh, I remember him. He had such curly hair when he was born."

"He's a martyr, too," says mum quietly.

"And this is my third son. My baby. My beautiful Ahmed. He would be eighteen," she whispers.

"Yes. I remember when he first started school."

"He's a martyr also," says mum with tears in her eyes.

After a pause and a deep sigh, the second Muslim mother looks wistfully at the photographs and says, "They blow up so fast, don't they?"

———★———

President Felipe Calderon of Mexico has announced that Mexico will not participate in the Beijing Summer Olympics.

He stated: "Casi cada uno que puede funcionar, saltar, o la nadada ha salido ya del pais."

Translation: "Pretty much everyone who can run, jump, or swim has already left the country.

—★—

2008 Version of The Little Red Hen

Once upon a time, on a farm in Virginia, there was a little red hen that scratched about the barnyard until she uncovered quite a few grains of wheat. She called all of her Democrat neighbors together and said, "If we plant this wheat, we shall have bread to eat. Who will help me plant it?"

"Not I," said the cow.

"Not I," said the duck.

"Not I," said the pig.

"Not I," said the goose.

"Then I will do it by myself," said the little red hen, and so she did. The wheat grew very tall and ripened into golden grain. "Who will help me reap my wheat?"

"Not I," said the duck.

"Out of my classification," said the pig.

"I'd lose my seniority," said the cow.

"I'd lose my unemployment compensation," said the goose.

"Then I will do it by myself," said the little red hen, and so she did. At last it came time to bake the bread. "Who will help me bake the bread?"

"That would be overtime for me," said the cow.

"I'd lose my welfare benefits," said the duck.

"I'm a dropout and never learned how," said the pig.

"If I'm to be the only helper, that's discrimination," said the goose.

"Then I will do it by myself," said the little red hen. She baked five loaves and held them up for all of her neighbors to see. They wanted some and, in fact, demanded a share. But the little red hen said, "No, I shall eat all five loaves."

"Excess profits!" cried the cow. (Nancy Pelosi)

"Capitalist leech!" screamed the duck. (Barbara Boxer)

"I demand equal rights!" yelled the goose. (Jesse Jackson)

The pig just grunted in disdain. (Ted Kennedy)

And they all painted "Unfair!" picket signs and marched around and around the little red hen, shouting obscenities.

Then the farmer Obama came. He said to the little red hen, "You must not be so greedy."

"But I earned the bread," said the little red hen.

"Exactly," said Barack the farmer. "That is what makes our free enterprise system so wonderful. Anyone in the barnyard can earn as much as he wants.

But under our modern government regulations, the productive workers must divide the fruits of their labor with those who are lazy and idle."

And they all lived happily ever after, including the little red hen, who smiled and clucked, "I am grateful, for now I truly understand."

But her neighbors became quite disappointed in her. She never again baked bread because she joined the "party" and got her bread free. And all the Democrats smiled. "Fairness" had been established.

Individual initiative had died, but nobody noticed; perhaps no one cared…so long as there was free bread that "the rich" were paying for.

Bill Clinton is getting twelve million dollars for his memoirs.

Hillary got eight million dollars for hers.

That's twenty million dollars for the memories from two people, who for eight years, repeatedly testified, under oath, that they couldn't remember anything.

Is this a great barnyard or what?

———★———

A Modern Version of Genesis

God was missing for six days. Eventually, Michael, the Archangel, found Him, resting on the seventh day. He inquired, "Where have you been?"

God smiled deeply and proudly pointed downwards through the clouds. "Look, Michael, look what I've made."

Archangel Michael looked puzzled, and said, "What is it?"

"It's a planet," replied God, "and I've put life on it. I'm going to call it Earth and it's going to be a place to test balance."

"Balance?" inquired Michael. "I'm still confused."

God explained, pointing to different parts of earth. "For example, northern Europe will be a place of great opportunity and wealth, while southern Europe is going to be poor.

"Over there I've placed a continent of white people, and over there is a continent of black people. Balance in all things," God continued pointing to different countries.

"This one will be extremely hot, while this one will be very cold and covered in ice."

The Archangel, impressed by God's work, then pointed to a land area and said, "What's that one?"

"That's Washington State, the most glorious place on earth. There are beautiful mountains, rivers and streams, lakes, forests, hills, and plains. The people from Washington State are going to be handsome, modest, intelligent, and humorous, and they are going to travel the world. They will be extremely sociable, hardworking, high achieving, and they will be known throughout the world as diplomats, carriers of peace, and producers of software!"

Michael gasped in wonder and admiration, and then asked, "But what about balance, God? You said there would be balance."

God smiled. "There is another Washington. Wait 'till you see the idiots I put there."

Solution to Airline Woes

Dump male flight attendants. No one wanted them in the first place.

Replace female flight attendants with good-looking strippers! What the hell— they don't even serve food any more, so what's the loss?

The strippers would at least triple the alcohol sales and get a "party atmosphere" going in the cabin. And, of course, every businessman in this country would start flying again, hoping to see naked women.

Because of the tips, female flight attendants wouldn't need a salary, thus saving even more money. I suspect tips would be so good that we could charge the women for working the plane and have them kick back 20 percent of the tips, including lap dances and "special services."

Muslims would be afraid to get on the planes for fear of seeing naked women. Hijackings would come to a screeching halt, and the airline industry would see record revenues.

This is definitely a win-win situation if we handle it right—a golden opportunity to turn a liability into an asset. Why didn't Bush think of this? Why do I still have to do everything myself?

Sincerely,
Bill Clinton

John the farmer was in the fertilized egg business. He had several hundred young layers (hens), called "pullets," and ten roosters, whose job it was to fertilize the eggs.

The farmer kept records and any rooster that didn't perform went into the soup pot and was replaced. That took an awful lot of his time, so he bought a set of tiny bells and attached them to his roosters. Each bell had a different tone so John could tell from a distance, which rooster was performing. Now he could sit on the porch and fill out an efficiency report simply by listening to the bells.

The farmer's favorite rooster was old Butch, a very fine specimen he was, too. But on this particular morning John noticed old Butch's bell hadn't rung at all! John went to investigate. The other roosters were chasing pullets, bells-a-ringing. The pullets, hearing the roosters coming, would run for cover.

But to farmer John's amazement, old Butch had his bell in his beak, so it couldn't ring. He'd sneak up on a pullet, do his job, and walk on to the next one. John was so proud of old Butch, he entered him in the Renfrew County Fair, and he became an overnight sensation among the judges.

The restult: the judges not only awarded old Butch the "No Bell Piece Prize," but they awarded him the "Pulletsurprise" as well.

Clearly old Butch was a politician in the making: who else but a politician could figure out how to win two of the most highly coveted awards on our planet by being the best at sneaking up on the populace and screwing them when they weren't paying attention.

Vote carefully this year...the bells are not always audible.

———★———

I was depressed last night so I rang a suicide hot-line. I was transferred to an out-sourced call center in Pakistan. I told them I was suicidal. They got all excited and asked if I could drive a truck.

———★———

The local bar was so sure that its bartender was the strongest man around that they offered a standing $1,000 bet. The bartender would squeeze a lemon until all the juice ran into a glass and hand the lemon to a patron. Anyone who could squeeze one more drop of juice out would win the money. Many people had tried over time (weight-lifters, longshoremen, etc.) but nobody could do it.

One day this scrawny little man came into the bar, wearing thick glasses and a polyester suit, and said in a tiny, squeaky voice, "I'd like to try the bet." After the laughter had died down, the bartender said okay, grabbed a lemon, and squeezed away. Then he handed the wrinkled remains of the rind to the little man.

But the crowd's laughter turned to total silence as the man clenched his fist around the lemon and six drops fell into the glass. As the crowd cheered, the bartender paid the $1,000, and asked the little man, "What do you do for a living? Are you a lumberjack, a weight-lifter, or what?"

The man replied, "I work for the IRS."

———★———

Monkey Market

Once upon a time in a village, a man appeared and announced to the villagers that he would buy monkeys for $10 each. The villagers seeing that there were many monkeys around, went out to the forest, and started catching them. The man bought thousands at $10, and as supply started to diminish, the villagers stopped their effort. He further announced that he would now buy at $20.

This renewed the efforts of the villagers, and they started catching monkeys again. Soon the supply diminished even further, and people started going back to their farms.

The offer increased to $25 each, and the supply of monkeys became so little that it was an effort to even see a monkey, let alone catch it!

The man now announced that he would buy monkeys at $50! However, since he had to go to the city on some business, his assistant would now buy on his behalf.

In the absence of the man, the assistant told the villagers "Look at all these monkeys in the big cage that the man has collected. I will sell them to you at $35 and when the man returns from the city, you can sell them to him for $50 each."

The villagers rounded up with all their savings and bought all the monkeys. Then they never saw the man nor his assistant ever again, only monkeys everywhere!

Now you have a better understanding of how the stock market works.

———★———

A game warden was driving down the road when he came upon a young boy carrying a wild turkey under his arm. He stopped and asked the boy, "Where did you get that turkey?"

The boy replied, "What turkey?"

The game warden said, "That turkey you're carrying under your arm."

The boy looks down and said, "Well, lookee here, a turkey done roosted under my arm!"

The game warden said, "Now look, you know turkey season is closed, so whatever you do to that turkey, I'm going to do to you. If you break his leg, I'm gonna break your leg. If you break his wing, I'll break your arm. Whatever you do to him, I'll do to you. So, what are you gonna do with him?"

The little boy said, "I guess I'll just kiss his ass and let him go!"

———★———

How many members of the Bush administration does it take to change a light bulb? Answer: ten.

1. One to deny that a light bulb needs to be changed;

2. One to attack the patriotism of anyone who says the light bulb needs to be changed;

3. One to blame Clinton for burning out the light bulb;

4. One to tell the nations of the world that they are either for changing the light bulb or for eternal darkness;

5. One to give a billion dollar no-bid contract to Halliburton for the new light bulb;

6. One to arrange a photograph of Bush, dressed as a janitor, standing on a step ladder under the banner "Bulb Accomplished";

7. One administration insider to resign and in detail reveal how Bush was literally "in the dark" the whole time;

8. One to viciously smear number seven;

9. One surrogate to campaign on TV and at rallies on how George Bush has had a strong light-bulb-changing policy all along;

10. And finally, one to confuse Americans about the difference between screwing a light bulb and screwing the country.

The George W. Bush Presidential Library is now in the planning stages. You'll want to be the first at your corporation to make a contribution to this great man's legacy. The library will include:

The Hurricane Katrina Room, which is still under construction.

The Alberto Gonzales Room, where you can't remember anything.

The Texas Air National Guard Room, where you don't have to even show up.

The Walter Reed Hospital Room, where they don't let you in.

The Guantanamo Bay Room, where they don't let you out.

The Weapons of Mass Destruction Room (which no one has been able to find).

The Iraq War Room. After you complete your first tour, they make you go back for a second, third, fourth, and sometimes fifth tour.

The Dick Cheney Room, in the famous undisclosed location, complete with shooting gallery.

The National Debt room, which is huge and has no ceiling.

The "Tax Cut" Room, which is only accessible to the wealthy.

The "Economy" Room, which is in the toilet.

The Environmental Conservation Room, which is empty.

The "Drug Plan" Room, which they're still trying to figure out.

The Immigration Reform Room complete with undocumented attendants.

Plans also include: The K-Street Project Gift Shop where you can buy (or just steal) an election.

The Airport Men's Room, where you can meet some of your favorite Republican senators.

Plans also include: The Supremes Gift Shop–where you can buy (or just steal) an election.

The Oil Baron's Lounge (funded by excessive profits from ripping off the public.)

The "Decider Room" complete with dart board, magic eight-ball, Ouija board, dice, coins, and straws.

Last, but not least, there will be an entire floor devoted to a seven-eighth-scale model of the president's ego.

To highlight the president's accomplishments, the museum will have an electron microscope to help you locate them. There will be a movie theater where you can view film clips of George landing on a carrier and declaring the Iraqi War to be over.

When asked, President Bush said that he didn't care so much about the individual exhibits as long as his museum was better than his father's.

Admission: Republicans–free; Democrats–$1,000 or three Euros (doesn't matter since none are going there anyway!)

This one is politically correct!

Baskin Robbins is introducing a new ice cream in honor of our new president:

"Barocky Road." It's half vanilla, half chocolate, surrounded by fruits and nuts!

——★——

My dog sleeps about twenty hours a day. She has her food prepared for her. She can eat whenever she wants, twenty-four/seven/365. Her meals are provided at no cost to her. She visits the doctor once a year for her checkup, and again during the year if any medical needs arise. For this she pays nothing and nothing is required of her. She lives in a nice neighborhood in a house that is much larger than she needs, but she is not required to do any upkeep. If she makes a mess, someone else cleans it up. She has her choice of luxurious places to sleep. She receives these accommodations absolutely free. She is living like a queen and has absolutely no expenses whatsoever. All of her costs are picked up by others who go out and earn a living every day. I was just thinking about all this, and suddenly it hit me like a brick in the head, Holy Cow! My dog is a democrat!

It was once said that a black man would be president when pigs flew. Well behold, 100 days into his presidency, swine flu.

———★———

Our troops in Afghanistan prove they've retained their sense of humor with the following:

You May Be A Taliban If...

- You refine heroin for a living, but you have a moral objection to beer.

- You own a $3,000 machine gun and $5,000 rocket launcher, but you can't afford shoes.

- You have more wives than teeth.

- You wipe your butt with your bare left hand, but consider bacon "unclean."

- You think vests come in two styles: bulletproof and suicide.

- You can't think of anyone you haven't declared Jihad against.

- You consider television dangerous but routinely carry explosives in your clothing.

- You were amazed to discover that cell phones have uses other than setting off roadside bombs.

- You have nothing against women and think every man should own at least two.

- You've always had a crush on your neighbor's goat.

———★———

On July 8, 1947, a little over sixty years ago, witnesses claim that an unidentified flying object (UFO) with five aliens aboard, crashed onto a sheep and cattle ranch just outside Roswell, New Mexico. This is a well-known incident that many say has long been covered up by the U.S. Air Force and other federal agencies and organizations.

However, what you may *not* know is that in the month of April 1948, nine months after that historic day, the following people were born:

Albert A. Gore Jr., Hillary Rodham, John F. Kerry, William J. Clinton, Howard Dean, Nancy Pelosi, Dianne Feinstein, Charles E. Schumer, and Barbara Boxer.

See what happens when aliens breed with sheep? No wonder all these politicians support bills to help illegal aliens!

———★———

A Harley rider is passing the zoo when he sees a little girl leaning into the lion's cage. Suddenly, the lion grabs her by the cuff of her jacket and tries to pull her inside to slaughter her, under the eyes of her screaming parents.

The biker jumps off his bike, runs to the cage, and hits the lion square on the nose with a powerful punch. Whimpering from the pain, the lion jumps back letting go of the girl, and the biker brings her to her terrified parents, who thank him endlessly.

A New York Times reporter has watched the whole event. The reporter says, "Sir, this was the most gallant and brave thing I've ever seen a man do in my whole life."

The biker replies, "Why, it was nothing, really, the lion was behind bars. I just saw this little kid in danger, and acted as I felt right."

The reporter says, "Well, I'm a journalist from the New York Times, and tomorrow's paper will have this story on the front page. So, what do you do for a living and what political affiliation do you have?"

The biker replies, "I'm a U.S. Marine and a Republican."

The following morning the biker buys The New York Times to see if it indeed brings news of his actions, and reads, on front page:

"U.S. Marine Assaults African Immigrant And Steals His Lunch."

————★————

Aircraft in the Persian Gulf AOR are required to give the Iranian Air Defense Radar (military) a ten-minute heads up if they will be transiting Iranian airspace. A pilot overheard this conversation on the VHF Guard (emergency) frequency 121.5 MHz while flying from Europe to Dubai. Read the conversation below:

Iranian Air Defense Radar: "Unknown aircraft you are in Iranian airspace. Identify yourself."

U.S. Aircraft: "This is a United States aircraft. I am in Iraqi airspace."

Iranian Air Defense Radar: "You are in Iranian airspace. If you do not depart our airspace we will launch interceptor aircraft!"

U.S. Aircraft: "This is a United States Marine Corps FA-18 fighter. Send 'em up. I'll wait!"

Iranian Air Defense Radar: (no response…)

———★———

The Economy Is So Bad That…

I got a pre-declined credit card in the mail.

I ordered a burger at McDonald's and the kid behind the counter asked, "Can you afford fries with that?"

CEOs are now playing miniature golf.

If the bank returns your check marked "Insufficient Funds," you call them and ask if they meant you or them.

Hot Wheels and Matchbox stocks are trading higher than GM.

Parents in Beverly Hills fired their nannies and learned their children's names.

A truckload of Americans was caught sneaking into Mexico.

Dick Cheney took his stockbroker hunting.

Motel Six won't leave the light on anymore.

Exxon-Mobil laid off twenty-five congressmen.

A stripper was killed when her audience showered her with rolls of pennies while she danced.

I saw a Mormon with only one wife.

McDonald's is selling the 1/4 ouncer.

Angelina Jolie adopted a child from America.

My cousin had an exorcism but couldn't afford to pay for it, and they re-possessed her!

A picture is now only worth 200 words.

When Bill and Hillary travel together, they now have to share a room.

The Treasure Island casino in Las Vegas is now managed by Somali pirates.

———★———

Congress says they are looking into this Bernie Madoff scandal. Oh, great! The guy who made $50 billion disappear is being investigated by the people who made $1.5 trillion disappear!

———★———

Sometime this year, we taxpayers will again receive an Economic Stimulus payment. This is a very exciting program.

I'll explain it using the Q and A format:

Q. What is an Economic Stimulus payment?
A. It is money that the federal government will send to taxpayers.

Q. Where will the government get this money?
A. From taxpayers.

Q. So the government is giving me back my own money?
A. Only a smidgen.

Q. What is the purpose of this payment?
A. The plan is for you to use the money to purchase a high-definition TV set, thus stimulating the economy.

Q. But isn't that stimulating the economy of Asia?
A. Shut up or you don't get your check.

———★———

How to Spend Your Stimulus Check

Below is some helpful advice on how to best help the US economy by spending your stimulus check wisely:

1. If you spend the stimulus money at Walmart, your money will go to China.

2. If you spend it on gasoline, your money will go to Saudi Arabia.

3. If you purchase a computer, it will go to India.

4. If you purchase fruit and vegetables, it will go to Mexico, Honduras, or Guatemala.

5. If you buy a car, it will go to Japan or Korea.

6. If you purchase useless plastic stuff, it will go to Taiwan.

7. If you pay off your credit cards, or buy stock, it will go to pay management bonuses and be hidden in offshore accounts.

Or, you can keep the money in America by:

1. Spending it at yard sales or flea markets; or

2. Going to baseball or football games; or

3. Hiring prostitutes; or

4. Buying cheap beer; or

5. Getting tattoos.

These are the only wholly American owned businesses currently operating in the U.S.

Conclusion:

The best way to stimulate the economy is to go to a ball game with a prostitute that you met at a yard sale and drink beer all day until you're drunk enough to go get tattooed. Sad but this is probably pretty accurate.

———★———

A man owned a small ranch near San Antonio. The Texas Department of Labor claimed he was not paying proper wages to his help and sent an agent out to interview him. "I need a list of your employees and how much you pay them," demanded the agent.

Well," replied the farmer, "there's my farm hand who's been with me for three years. I pay him two hundred dollars a week plus free room and board. The cook has been here for eighteen months, and I pay her one hundred and fifty dollars per week plus free room and board. Then there's the half-wit. He works about eighteen hours every day and does about ninety percent of all the work around here. He makes about ten dollars per week, pays his own room and board, and I buy him a bottle of bourbon every Saturday night. He also sleeps with my wife occasionally."

"That's the guy I want to talk to…the half-wit," says the agent.

"That would be me," replied the rancher.

——★——

Two radical Arab terrorists boarded a flight out of London. One took a window seat and the other sat next to him in the middle seat. Just before takeoff, a Rabbi sat down in the aisle seat.

After takeoff, the Rabbi kicked his shoes off, wiggled his toes and was settling in when the Arab in the window seat said, "I need to get up and get a coke."

"Don't get up," said the Rabbi, "I'm in the aisle seat, I'll get it for you."

As soon as he left, one of the Arabs picked up the Rabbi's shoe and spat in it. When the Rabbi returned with the coke, the other Arab said, "That looks good, I'd really like one, too."

Again, the Rabbi obligingly went to fetch it. While he was gone the other Arab picked up the rabbi's other shoe and spat in it. When the rabbi returned, they all sat back and enjoyed the flight.

As the plane was landing, the Rabbi slipped his feet into his shoes and knew immediately what had happened. He leaned over and asked his Arab neighbors, "Why does it have to be this way? How long must this go on? This fighting between our nations? This hatred? This animosity? This spitting in shoes and pissing in cokes?"

———★———

Let me see if I got this right.

If you cross the North Korean border illegally you get twelve years hard labor.

If you cross the Iranian border illegally you are detained indefinitely.

If you cross the Afghan border illegally, you get shot.

If you cross the Saudi Arabian border illegally you will be jailed.

If you cross the Chinese border illegally you may never be heard from again.

If you cross the Venezuelan border illegally you will be branded a spy and your fate will be sealed.

If you cross the Cuban border illegally you will be thrown into political prison to rot.

If you cross the U.S. border illegally you get

1. a job,

2. a drivers license,

3. social security card,

4. welfare,

5. food stamps,

6. credit cards,

7. subsidized rent or a loan to buy a house,

8. free education,

9. free health care,

10. a lobbyist in Washington

11. billions of dollars worth of public documents printed in your language

12. and the right to carry your country's flag while you protest that you don't get enough respect

———★———

I just wanted to make sure I had a firm grasp on the situation…

I recently asked my friends' little girl what she wanted to be when she grows up.

She said she wanted to be president some day. Both of her parents, liberal Democrats, were standing there.

So I asked her, "If you were president what would be the first thing you would do?"

She replied, "I'd give food and houses to all the homeless people."

Her parents beamed with pride.

"Wow…what a worthy goal," I told her. "But you don't have to wait until you're president to do that. You can come over to my house and mow the lawn, pull weeds, and sweep my yard, and I'll pay you fifty dollars.

"Then I'll take you over to the grocery store where the homeless guy hangs out, and you can give him the fifty dollars to use toward food and a new house."

She thought that over for a few seconds, and then she looked me straight in the eye and asked, "Why doesn't the homeless guy come over and do the work, and you can just pay him the fifty dollars directly?"

I said, "Welcome to the Republican Party."

Her parents still aren't speaking to me.

———★———

George Bush, Queen Elizabeth, and Vladimir Putin all die and go to hell. While there, they spy a red phone and ask what the phone is for. The devil tells them it is for calling back to Earth.

Putin asks to call Russia and talks for five minutes. When he was finished the devil informs him that the cost is a million dollars, so Putin writes him a check.

Next Queen Elizabeth calls England and talks for thirty minutes. When she was finished the devil informs her that cost is six million dollars, so Queen Elizabeth writes him a check.

Finally George Bush gets his turn and talks for four hours. When he was finished the devil informed him that there would be no charge for the call and feel free to call the USA anytime.

When Putin hears this he goes ballistic and asks the devil why Bush got to call the USA free.

The devil replied, "Since Obama became president of the USA, the country has gone to hell, so it's a local call."

———★———

Top ten indicators that your employer has changed to Obama's Healthcare:

10. Your annual breast exam is done at Hooters.

9. Directions to your doctor's office include "Take a left when you enter the trailer park."

8. The tongue depressors taste faintly of fudge or orange popsicles

7. The only proctologist in the plan is "Gus" from Roto-Rooter.

6. The only item listed under Preventative Care Coverage is "an apple a day."

5. Your primary care physician is wearing the pants you gave to Goodwill last month.

4. "The patient is responsible for 200 percent of out-of-network charges," is not a typographical error.

3. The only expense covered 100 percent is, "Embalming."

2. Your Prozac comes in different colors with little M's on them.

And the number one sign you've joined Obama's health care plan:

1. You ask for Viagra, and they give you a popsicle stick and duct tape.

———★———

Air Force One crashed in the middle of rural America. Panic stricken, the local sheriff mobilized and descended on the farm in force. When they got there, the disaster was clear. The aircraft was totally destroyed with only a burned hulk left smoldering in a tree line that bordered a farm. The sheriff and his men entered the smoking mess but could find no remains of anyone, including the president. They spotted a lone farmer plowing a field not too far away as if nothing at all happened. They hurried over to the man's tractor.

"Hank," the sheriff yelled, panting and out of breath, "did you see this terrible accident happen?"

"Yep. Sure did," the farmer mumbled unconcernedly, cutting off the tractor's engine.

"Do you realize that is the airplane of the president of the United States ?"

"Yep."

"Were there any survivors?"

"Nope. They's all kilt straight out," the farmer answered. "I done buried them all myself. Took me most of the morning…"

"President Obama is dead?" the sheriff shouted.

"Well," the farmer grumbled, restarting his tractor, "he kept a-saying he wasn't, but you know how bad that idiot lies."

———★———

Over 5,000 years ago, Moses said to the children of Israel, "Pick up your shovel, mount your asses and camels, and I will lead you to the Promised Land."

Nearly 75 years ago, Roosevelt said, "Lay down your shovels, sit on your asses, and light up a camel, this is the Promised Land."

Now Obama has stolen your shovel, taxed your asses, raised the price of camels, and mortgaged the Promised Land!

———★———

Al Qaeda On Strike

Muslim suicide bombers in Britain are set to begin a three-day strike on Monday in a dispute over the number of virgins they are entitled to in the afterlife. Emergency talks with Al Qaeda have so far failed to produce an agreement. The unrest began last Tuesday when Al Qaeda announced that the number of virgins a suicide bomber would receive after his death will be cut by 25 percent this February from seventy-two to only fifty-four. The rationale for the cut was the increase in recent years of the number of suicide bombings and a subsequent shortage of virgins in the afterlife. The suicide bombers' union, the British Organization of Occupational Martyrs (or B.O.O.M.) responded with a statement that this was unacceptable to its members and immediately balloted for strike action.

General Secretary Abdullah Amir told the press, "Our members are literally working themselves to death in the cause of Jihad. We don't ask for much in return but to be treated like this is like a kick in the teeth."

Speaking from his shed in Tipton in the West Midlands in which he currently resides, Al Qaeda chief executive Osama bin Laden explained, "We sympathize with our workers' concerns, but Al Qaeda is simply not in a position to meet their demands. They are simply not accepting the realities of modern-day Jihad in a competitive marketplace.

"Thanks to Western depravity, there is now a chronic shortage of virgins in the afterlife. It's a straight choice between reducing expenditure and laying people off. I don't like cutting wages, but I'd hate to have to tell three thousand of my staff that they won't be able to blow themselves up."

Spokespersons for the union in the Northeast of England, Ireland, Wales, and the entire Australian continent stated that the strike would not affect their operations as "there are no virgins in our areas anyway."

Apparently the drop in the number of suicide bombings has been put down to the emergence of the Scottish singing star Susan Boyle—now that Muslims know what a virgin looks like, they are not so keen on going to paradise.

———★———

Jose and Carlos are both beggars begging in different parts of town. They both beg for four hours a day. Carlos only brings home $10 to $20 each day, but Jose brings home a suitcase full of ten-dollar bills every day.

Jose drives a Mercedes, lives in a mortgage-free house, and has a lot of money to spend.

"Hey, amigo," Carlos says to Jose, "I work just as long and hard as you do, so how come you bring home a suitcase full of ten-dollar bills every day?"

Jose says, "Look at your sign, what does it say?"

"I have no work, a wife, and six kids to support. What's wrong with that?" Carlos asks him.

"No wonder you only get ten to twenty dollars a day!" Jose responds.

Carlos says, "All right, what does your sign say?"

Jose replies, "It says I only need ten more dollars to get back to Mexico."

Let's put the seniors in jail, and the criminals in a nursing home.

This way the seniors would have access to showers, hobbies, and walks, they'd receive unlimited free prescriptions, dental and medical treatment, wheelchairs etc. and they'd receive money instead of paying it out.

They would have constant video monitoring, so they could be helped instantly if they fell or needed assistance. Bedding would be washed twice a week, and all clothing would be ironed and returned to them.

A guard would check on them every twenty minutes, and bring their meals and snacks to their cell.

They would have family visits in a suite built for that purpose. They would have access to a library, weight room, spiritual counseling, pool, and education. Simple clothing, shoes, slippers, pajamas, and legal aid would be free on request. Private, secure rooms for all, with an exercise outdoor yard with gardens.

Each senior could have a PC, a TV, radio, and daily phone calls. There would be a board of directors to hear complaints and the guards would have a code of conduct that would be strictly adhered to.

The "criminals" would get cold food, be left all alone and unsupervised, lights off at 8:00 p.m., and showers once a week. They would live in a tiny room and pay $5,000.00 per month and have no hope of ever getting out. Justice for all!

An easy guide to keeping political news in perspective…

The *Wall Street Journal* is read by the people who run the country.

The *Washington Post* is read by people who think they run the country.

The *New York Times* is read by people who think they should run the country, and who are very good at crossword puzzles.

USA Today is read by people who think they ought to run the country but don't really understand The *New York Times*. They do, however, like their statistics shown in pie charts.

The *Los Angeles Times* is read by people who wouldn't mind running the country, if they could find the time—and if they didn't have to leave Southern California to do it.

The *Boston Globe* is read by people whose parents used to run the country.

The *New York Daily News* is read by people who aren't too sure who's running the country and don't really care as long as they can get a seat on the train.

The *New York Post* is read by people who don't care who is running the country as long as they do something really scandalous, preferably while intoxicated.

The *Miami Herald* is read by people who are running another country, but need the baseball scores.

The *San Francisco Chronicle* is read by people who aren't sure if there is a country or that anyone is running it; but if so, they oppose all that they stand for. There are occasional exceptions if the leaders are handicapped, minority, feminist, atheist dwarfs who also happen to be illegal aliens from any other country or galaxy, provided of course, that they are not Republicans.

The *National Enquirer* is read by people trapped in line at the grocery store.

The *Seattle Times* is read by people who have recently caught a fish and need something to wrap it in.

———★———

A young woman was about to finish her first year of college. Like so many others her age, she considered herself to be very liberal, and among other liberal ideals, was very much in favor of higher taxes to support more government programs, in other words redistribution of wealth.

She was deeply ashamed that her father was a rather staunch conservative, a feeling she openly expressed. Based on the lectures that she had participated in, and the occasional chat with a professor, she felt that her father had for years harbored an evil, selfish desire to keep what he thought should be his.

One day she was challenging her father on his opposition to higher taxes on the rich and the need for more government programs.

The self-professed objectivity proclaimed by her professors had to be the truth, and she indicated so to her father. He responded by asking how she was doing in school.

Taken aback, she answered rather haughtily that she had a 4.0 GPA and let him know that it was tough to maintain, insisting that she was taking a very difficult course load and was constantly studying, which left her no time to go out and party like other people she knew. She didn't even have time for a boyfriend and didn't really have many college friends because she spent all her time studying.

Her father listened and then asked, "How is your friend Audrey doing?"

She replied, "Audrey is barely getting by. All she takes are easy classes, she never studies, and she barely has a 2.0 GPA. She is so popular on campus. College for her is a blast. She's always invited to all the parties and lots of times she doesn't even show up for classes because she's too hung over."

Her wise father asked his daughter, "Why don't you go to the dean's office and ask him to deduct 1.0 off your GPA and give it to your friend who only has a 2.0. That way you will both have a 3.0 GPA and certainly that would be a fair and equal distribution of GPA."

The daughter, visibly shocked by her father's suggestion, angrily fired back, "That's a crazy idea, how would that be fair! I've worked really hard for my grades! I've invested a lot of time, and a lot of hard work! Audrey has done next to nothing toward her degree. She played while I worked my tail off!"

The father slowly smiled, winked and said gently, "Welcome to the conservative side of the fence."

If you ever wondered what side of the fence you sit on, this is a great test!

If a conservative doesn't like guns, he doesn't buy one.

If a liberal doesn't like guns, he wants all guns outlawed.

If a conservative is a vegetarian, he doesn't eat meat.

If a liberal is a vegetarian, he wants all meat products banned for everyone.

If a conservative is down-and-out, he thinks about how to better his situation.

A liberal wonders who is going to take care of him.

If a conservative doesn't like a talk show host, he switches channels.

Liberals demand that those they don't like be shut down.

If a conservative is a non-believer, he doesn't go to church.

A liberal non-believer wants any mention of God and Jesus silenced.

If a conservative decides he needs health care, he goes about shopping for it, or may choose a job that provides it.

A liberal demands that the rest of us pay for his.

How To Properly Place New Employees

1. Put 400 bricks in a closed room.

2. Put your new employees in the room and close the door.

3. Leave them alone and come back after six hours.

4. Then analyze the situation:

    a. If they are counting the bricks, put them in the accounting department.

    b. If they are recounting them, put them in auditing.

    c. If they have messed up the whole place with the bricks, put them in engineering.

    d. If they are arranging the bricks in some strange order, put them in planning.

    e. If they are throwing the bricks at each other, put them in operations.

    f. If they are sleeping, put them in security.

    g. If they have broken the bricks into pieces, put them in information technology.

    h. If they are sitting idle, put them in human resources.

i. If they say they have tried different combinations, they are looking for more, yet not a brick has been moved, put them in sales.

j. If they have already left for the day, put them in marketing.

k. If they are staring out of the window, put them in strategic planning.

l. If they are talking to each other, and not a single brick has been moved, congratulate them and put them in top management.

m. Finally, if they have surrounded themselves with bricks in such a way that they can neither be seen nor heard from, put them in government.

———★———

I was eating lunch on the twentieth of February with my ten-year-old granddaughter, and I asked her, "What day is tomorrow?"

She said, "It's President's Day!"

She is a smart kid.

I asked, "What does President's Day mean?"

I was waiting for something about Washington or Lincoln...etc.

She replied, "President's Day is when President Obama steps out of the White House, and if he sees his shadow we have one more year of unemployment."

You know, it hurts when hot coffee spurts out your nose...

———★———

President Obama's approval ratings are so low now Kenyans are accusing him of being born in the United States.

———★———

On a Saturday afternoon, in Washington, D.C., an aide to House Speaker Nancy Pelosi visited the Bishop of the Catholic cathedral in D.C. He told the Cardinal that Nancy Pelosi would be attending the next day's Mass, and he asked if the Cardinal would kindly point out Pelosi to the congregation and say a few words that would include calling Pelosi a saint.

The Cardinal replied, "No. I don't really like the woman, and there are issues of conflict with the Catholic Church over certain of Pelosi's views."

Pelosi's aide then said, "Look. I'll write a check here and now for a donation of one hundred thousand dollars to your church if you'll just tell the congregation you see Pelosi as a saint."

The Cardinal thought about it and said, "Well, the church can use the money, so I'll work your request into tomorrow's sermon."

As Pelosi's aide promised, House Speaker Pelosi appeared for the Sunday worship and seated herself prominently at the forward left side of the center aisle.

As promised, at the start of his sermon, the Cardinal pointed out that Speaker Pelosi was present. The Cardinal went on to explain to the congregation, "While Speaker Pelosi's presence is probably an honor to some; the woman is not numbered among my personal favorite personages. Some of her most egregious views are contrary to tenets of the church, and she tends to flip-flop on many other issues. Nancy Pelosi is a petty, self-absorbed hypocrite, a thumb sucker, and a nitwit. Nancy Pelosi is also a serial liar, a cheat, and a thief. I must say Nancy Pelosi is the worst example of a Catholic I have ever personally witnessed. She married for money and is using her wealth to lie to the American people. She also has a reputation for shirking her Representative obligations both in Washington and in California. The woman is simply not to be trusted."

The Cardinal concluded, "But, when compared with President Obama, House Speaker Pelosi is a saint."

——★——

Congress says they are looking into this Bernard Madoff scandal. Oh Great! The guy who made $50 Billion disappear is being investigated by the people who made $1.5 Trillion disappear!

Sandy Rozelman

Dear scissors,

I feel your pain…no one wants to run with me either.

Sincerely,
Sarah Palin

— ★ —

Dear World,

Please stop freaking out about 2012. Our calendar ends there because some Spanish dirtbags invaded our country and we got a little busy okay?

Sincerely,
The Mayans

— ★ —

Dear White People,

Don't you just hate immigrants?

Sincerely,
Native Americans

— ★ —

The Wizard of Oz is seventy-two years old. Today, if Dorothy were to encounter men with no brains, no heart, and no balls, she wouldn't be in Oz. She'd be in Congress.

President Obama goes to a primary school to talk to the kids to get a little PR. After his talk he offers question time. One little boy puts up his hand and Obama asks him his name.

"Stanley," responds the little boy.

"And what is your question, Stanley?"

"I have four questions: first, why did the USA bomb Libya without the support of the Congress? Second, why are you president when John McCain got more votes? Third, whatever happened to Osama Bin Laden? Fourth, why are we so worried about gay-marriage when half of all Americans don't have health insurance?"

Just then, the bell rings for recess. Obama informs the kiddies that they will continue after recess.

When they resume Obama says, "Okay, where were we? Oh, that's right, question time. Who has a question?"

Another little boy puts up his hand. Obama points him out and asks him his name.

"Steve," he responds.

"And what is your question, Steve?"

"Actually, I have six questions. First, why did the USA bomb Libya without the support of the Congress? Second, why are you president when John McCain got more votes? Third, whatever happened to Osama Bin Laden? Fourth, why are we so worried about gay marriage when half of all Americans don't have health insurance? Fifth, why did the recess bell go off twenty minutes early? And sixth, what the f_ _k happened to Stanley?"

Watching the Republicans and the Democrats bicker over the U.S. debt is analogous to watching two drunks argue over a bar bill on the Titanic.

Having arrived at the gates of heaven, Barack Obama meets a man with a beard. "Are you Mohammed?" he asks. "No, my son, I am St. Peter. Mohammed is higher up." Peter then points to a ladder that rises into the clouds.

Delighted that Mohammed should be higher than St. Peter, Obama climbs the ladder in great strides, climbs up through the clouds, and comes into a room where he meets another bearded man. He asks again, "Are you Mohammed?"

"Why no," he answers, "I am Moses. Mohammed is higher still."

Exhausted, but with a heart full of joy, he climbs the ladder yet again.

He discovers a larger room where he meets an angelic-looking man with a beard. Full of hope, he asks again, "Are you Mohammed?"

"No, I am Jesus, the Christ. You will find Mohammed higher up."

Mohammed higher than Jesus! Man, oh man! Obama can hardly contain his delight and climbs and climbs ever higher. Once again, he reaches an even larger room where he meets this truly magnificent looking man with a silver white beard and once again repeats his question: "Are you Mohammed?" he gasps as he is by now, totally out of breath from all his climbing.

"No, my son, I am Almighty God, the Alpha and the Omega, but you look exhausted. Would you like a cup of coffee?"

Obama says, "Yes, please!" As God looks behind him, he claps his hands and yells out: "Hey, Mohammed, two coffees!"

———★———

Made in...

John started the day early having set his alarm clock MADE IN JAPAN for 6:00 a.m. While his coffeepot MADE IN CHINA was perking, he shaved with his electric razor MADE IN HONG KONG.

He put on a dress shirt MADE IN SRI LANKA, designer jeans MADE IN SINGAPORE and tennis shoes MADE IN KOREA.

After cooking his breakfast in his new electric skillet MADE IN INDIA he sat down with his calculator MADE IN MEXICO to see how much he could spend today. After setting his watch MADE IN TAIWAN to the radio MADE IN INDIA he got in his car MADE IN GERMANY filled it with gas from SAUDI ARABIA and continued his search for a good paying American Job.

At the end of yet another discouraging and fruitless day checking his computer MADE IN MALAYSIA, John decided to relax for a while.

He put on his sandals MADE IN BRAZIL, poured himself a glass of wine MADE IN FRANCE and turned on his TV MADE IN INDONESIA, and then wondered why he can't find a good paying job in America.

And now he's hoping he can get help from a president made in Kenya.

———★———

It has just been reported that the head gardener at the White House has been dismissed after twenty-eight years of loyal service to the many US presidents. When interviewed the elderly, Caucasian gardener protested his innocence and said, "All I know is I was walking past the Oval Office, and I yelled out to my assistants, 'Has anyone seen the spade and the hoe?' The next thing I knew I was fired."

———★———

Cash for Clunkers…Can we trade in Congress?

———★———

A crusty old Marine Sergeant Major found himself at a gala event hosted by a local liberal arts college. There was no shortage of extremely young, idealistic ladies in attendance, one of whom approached the Sergeant Major for conversation.

"Excuse me, Sergeant Major, but you seem to be a very serious man. Is something bothering you?"

"Negative, ma'am. Just serious by nature."

The young lady looked at his awards and decorations and said, "It looks like you have seen a lot of action."

"Yes, ma'am, a lot of action."

The young lady, tiring of trying to start up a conversation, said, "You know, you should lighten up. Relax and enjoy yourself."

The Sergeant Major just stared at her in his serious manner.

Finally the young lady said, "You know, I hope you don't take this the wrong way, but when is the last time you had sex?"

"Nineteen fifty-five, ma'am."

"Well, there you are. No wonder you're so serious. You really need to chill out! I mean, no sex since Nineteen fifty-five! She took his hand and led him to a private room where she proceeded to "relax" him several times.

Afterwards, panting for breath, she leaned against his bare chest and said, "Wow, you sure didn't forget much since 1955."

The Sergeant Major said in his serious voice, after glancing at his watch, "I hope not; it's only twenty-one thirty now."

Gotta love military time.

Young Dave moved to Maine and bought a donkey from a farmer for $100.00. The farmer agreed to deliver the donkey the next day. The next day he drove up and said, "Sorry, son, but I have some bad news, the donkey died."

Dave replied, "Well, then just give me my money back."

The farmer said, "Can't do that. I went and spent it already."

Dave said, "Okay, then, just bring me the dead donkey."

The farmer asked, "What ya gonna do with him?"

Dave said, "I'm going to raffle him off."

The farmer said, "You can't raffle off a dead donkey!"

Dave said, "Sure I can. Watch me. I just won't tell anybody he's dead."

A month later, the farmer met up with Dave and asked, "What happened with that dead donkey?"

Dave said, "I raffled him off. I sold five hundred tickets at two dollars a piece and made a profit of nine hundred and ninety-eight dollars."

The farmer said, "Didn't anyone complain?"

Dave said, "Just the guy who won. So I gave him his two dollars back."

Dave now oversees the Bailout Program.

———★———

So you're a sick senior citizen and the government says there is no nursing home available for you, what do you do? Our plan gives everyone sixty-five years or older a gun and four bullets. You're allowed to shoot four congressmen. Of course, this means you'll be sent to prison where you will get:

Three meals a day plus room and board

Central heating and air conditioning

Healthcare, dental and vision

Health club and library

Theater and recreation rooms

As an added bonus, your kids can come and visit you as often as they do now. Guess who's paying for all this? The same government that just told you that they cannot afford to put you in a home.

Super Bonus: Because you're a prisoner, you don't have to pay any income taxes!

Is this a great country or what?

———★———

The English language has some wonderful collective nouns for the various groups of animals. For example, we are all familiar with a herd of cows, a flock of chickens, a school of fish, and a gaggle of geese.

Lesser-known words are a pride of lions, a murder of crows, an exaltation of larks, and a muster of storks.

Now consider a group of baboons. They are the loudest, most dangerous, destructive, obnoxious, viciously aggressive and unintelligent of all primates. And what is the appropriate noun for a group of baboons?

Believe it or not…a Congress!

Electile Dysfunction: the inability to become aroused over any of the choices for president put forth by either party in the 2012 election year.

———★———

The ship of state is the only known vessel that leaks from the top!

———★———

Divorce Agreement

We have stuck together since the late 1950s for the sake of the kids, but the whole of this latest election process has made me realize that I want a divorce. I know we tolerated each other for many years for the sake of future generations, but sadly, this relationship has clearly run its course.

Our two ideological sides of America cannot and will not ever agree on what is right for us all, so let's just end it on friendly terms. We can smile and chalk it up to irreconcilable differences and go our own way.

———★———

Obama goes on a state visit to Israel. While he is on a tour of Jerusalem, he has a fatal heart attack and dies.

The undertaker tells the US diplomats: "You can have him shipped home for one million dollars or you can bury him here for one hundred dollars."

The US diplomats go into a huddle and come back to the undertaker and tell him they want Obama flown home.

The undertaker is puzzled and asks: "Why would you spend one million dollars to get him home when it would be wonderful to be buried here and you would only spend one hundred dollars?"

One diplomat replied: "More than two thousand years ago a man died here, was buried here, and three days later he rose from the dead. We simply can't take that risk."

———★———

"Hi. This is Sarah Palin. Is Senator Lieberman in?"
"No, Governor. This is Rosh Hashanah."
"Well, hello, Rosh. Can I leave a message?"
(OY VEY!)

———★———

The IRS sent my tax return back! I guess it was because of my response to the question: "List all dependents?"

I replied:

"12 million illegal immigrants;

"3 million crack heads;

"42 million unemployable people on food stamps;

"2 million people in over 243 prisons;

"Half of Mexico and 535 fools in the US House and Senate."

Apparently, this was not an acceptable answer.

In a Purdue University classroom, the students and their professor were discussing the qualifications to be president of the United States. It was pretty simple. The candidate must be a natural born citizen of at least thirty-five years of age.

However, one girl in the class immediately started in on how unfair was the requirement to be a natural born citizen. In short, her opinion was that this requirement prevented many capable individuals from becoming president.

The class was taking it in and letting her rant, and not many jaws hit the floor when she wrapped up her argument by stating, "What makes a natural born citizen any more qualified to lead this country than one born by C-section?"

"They breed and walk among us."

———★———

From a show on Canadian TV, there was a black comedian who said he misses Bill Clinton.

"Yep, that's right. I miss Bill Clinton! He was the closest thing we ever got to having a real black man as president.

Number one–He played the sax.

Number two–He smoked weed.

Number three–He had his way with ugly white women.

Even now. Look at him. His wife works, and he doesn't! And, he gets a check from the government every month. Manufacturers announced today that they will be stocking America's shelves this week with "Clinton Soup," in honor of one of the nations' distinguished men. It consists primarily of a weenie in hot water.

Chrysler Corporation is adding a new car to its line to honor Bill Clinton. The Dodge Drafter will be built in Canada.

When asked what he thought about foreign affairs, Clinton replied, "I don't know, I never had one."

The Clinton revised judicial oath: "I solemnly swear to tell the truth as I know it, the whole truth as I believe it to be, and nothing but what I think you need to know."

Clinton will be recorded in history as the only president to do hanky-panky between the bushes.

———★———

Dear American Taxpayer,

For only the second time in my adult life, I am not ashamed of my country. I want to thank the hardworking American people for paying $242,000 for my vacation in Spain. My daughter Sasha, several long-time family friends, my personal staff and various guests had a wonderful time. Honestly, you just haven't lived until you have stayed in a $2,500.00 per night private three-story villa at a Five-Star luxury hotel.

Thank you also for the use of Air Force Two and the seventy Secret Service personnel who tagged along to be sure we were safe and cared for at all times.

By the way, if you happen to be visiting the Costa del Sol, I highly recommend the Buenaventura Plaza restaurant in Marbella; great lobster with rice and oysters! I'm ashamed to admit the lobsters we ate in Martha's Vineyard were not quite as tasty, but what can you do if you're not in Europe, you have to just grin and bear it?

Air Force Two (which costs $11,351 per hour to operate according to Government Accounting Office reports) only used 47,500 gallons of jet fuel for this trip and carbon emissions were a mere 1,031 tons of CO_2.

These are only rough estimates, but they are close. That's quite a carbon footprint as my good friend Al Gore would say, so we must ask the American citizens to drive smaller, more fuel-efficient cars and drive less, too, so we can lessen our combined carbon footprint.

I know times are hard and millions of you are struggling to put food on the table and trying to make ends meet. So I do appreciate your sacrifices and do hope you find work soon.

I was really exhausted after Barack took our family on a luxury vacation in Maine a few weeks ago. I just had to get away for a few days.

Cordially,
Michelle (Moochelle) Obama

P.S. Thank you as well for the $2 billion-trip to India from which we just returned!

P.SS. Thank you, too, for that vacation trip to Martha's Vineyard; it was fabulous.
And thanks for that second smaller jet that took our dog, Bo, to Martha's Vineyard so we and the children could have him with us while we were away from the White House for eleven days. After all, we couldn't take him on Air Force One because he might pee on some wires or something.

P.S.S.S. Oh, I almost forgot to say thanks also for our two-week trip to Hawaii at Christmas. That 7,000-square-foot-house was great!

P.S.S.S.S don't forget my ski trip to Vail this winter and now the girls and I are in Africa with my mom. All this while Barack golf's and campaigns to keep my trips coming for the next four years!

Love ya! Remember, we all have to share the pain of these economic times equally!

Love to 'redistribute' (share) the wealth.

————★————

Dear 2012,

So I hear the best rapper is white and the president is black?
WTF happened?

Sincerely,
1985

————★————

Due to current economic conditions the light at the end of the tunnel has been turned off.